SCHOLASTIC

Grades 1–3

Partner Poems & Word Ladders
for Building Foundational Literacy Skills

DAVID L. HARRISON, TIMOTHY V. RASINSKI,
AND MARY JO FRESCH

Scholastic Inc. grants teachers permission to print and photocopy the reproducible pages from this book for classroom use. Purchase of this book entitles use of reproducibles by one teacher for one classroom only. No other part of this publication may be reproduced in whole or in part, or stored in a retrieval system, or transmitted in any form or by any means, electronic, mechanical, photocopying, recording, or otherwise, without written permission of the publisher. For information regarding permission, write to Scholastic Inc., 557 Broadway, New York, NY 10012.

Editor: Maria L. Chang
Cover design: Tannaz Fassihi
Cover and interior art: Julissa Mora; other images (76, 118): Shutterstock.com
Interior design: Maria Lilja

ISBN: 978-1-338-79289-8

Scholastic Inc., 557 Broadway, New York, NY 10012
Copyright © 2022 by David L. Harrison, Timothy V. Rasinski, and Mary Jo Fresch
Published by Scholastic Inc. All rights reserved.
Printed in the U.S.A.
First printing, January 2022.

1 2 3 4 5 6 7 8 9 10   40   30 29 28 27 26 25 24 23 22

Table of Contents

Introduction
Meet the Authors 6
What's in This Book 8
How to Use This Book 9

The 26 Phonograms

-ail
Partner Poem: Jail Break! 12
Word Ladders 1 and 2 13
Mini-Lesson: Write a Riddle 15

-ain
Partner Poem: The Muddy Drain Stain 16
Word Ladders 1 and 2 17
Mini-Lesson: Make a Word Search 19

-ake
Partner Poem: Saved by the Snake 20
Word Ladders 1 and 2 22
Mini-Lesson: Word Webs 24

-ale
Partner Poem: Don't Eat That! 25
Word Ladders 1 and 2 26
Mini-Lesson: Homophone Challenge 28

-ame
Partner Poem: The Night the Great Goat Came 29
Word Ladders 1 and 2 31
Mini-Lesson: Same as Similes 33

-ash
Partner Poem: The Odd Case of the Lash Hash 34
Word Ladders 1 and 2 35
Mini-Lesson: -ash Crossword 37

-ate
Partner Poem: Nate and Kate's Date 38
Word Ladders 1 and 2 40
Mini-Lesson: Hop Along 42

-aw
Partner Poem: The Oddest Crow 43
Word Ladders 1 and 2 44
Mini-Lesson: Draw a Word 46

-eat
Partner Poem: Starving in the Back Seat 47
Word Ladders 1 and 2 48
Mini-Lesson: Spoons for *-eats* 50

-eed
Partner Poem: Never Feed a Centipede 51
Word Ladders 1 and 2 53
Mini-Lesson: Connect 4 Phonograms 55

-ell
Partner Poem: The Shell at the Beach 56
Word Ladders 1 and 2 58
Mini-Lesson: What's My Number? 60

-est
Partner Poem: I Want to Be a Cowgirl 61
Word Ladders 1 and 2 62
Mini-Lesson: Guessing Game 64

-ew
Partner Poem: Just for "Ew" 65
Word Ladders 1 and 2 66
Mini-Lesson: Acrostic Sentences 68

-ice
Partner Poem: Beware of Mice 69
Word Ladders 1 and 2 70
Mini-Lesson: Going on a Word Hunt 72

-ick
Partner Poem: The Tick That Liked Cookies 73
Word Ladders 1 and 2 74
Mini-Lesson: Fish Stick 76

-ide
Partner Poem: Poor Clyde 77
Word Ladders 1 and 2 78
Mini-Lesson: Hide the Words 80

-ight
Partner Poem: My Wish Tonight 81
Word Ladders 1 and 2 82
Mini-Lesson: Word Construction 84

-ine
- Partner Poem: Careful, Little Fish 85
- Word Ladders 1 and 2 86
- Mini-Lesson: Four in a Line 88

-oat
- Partner Poem: How Not to Build a Boat 89
- Word Ladders 1 and 2 91
- Mini-Lesson: Word Organizer 93

-ock
- Partner Poem: Smelly Sock 94
- Word Ladders 1 and 2 95
- Mini-Lesson: Sock Match 97

-oke
- Partner Poem: An Artichoke Joke 98
- Word Ladders 1 and 2 99
- Mini-Lesson: Box the Words 101

-ore
- Partner Poem: The Bird That Snored 102
- Word Ladders 1 and 2 103
- Mini-Lesson: Ore Match 105

-out
- Partner Poem: Shout for Brussels Sprout 106
- Word Ladders 1 and 2 107
- Mini-Lesson: Shout It Out 109

-ow (long sound)
- Partner Poem: Rats, I Forgot! 110
- Word Ladders 1 and 2 112
- Mini-Lesson: Roll for -ow Words 114

-ow (short sound)
- Partner Poem: It's Too Late Now 115
- Word Ladders 1 and 2 116
- Mini-Lesson: Ow Swat 118

-oon/-ook/-oom
- Partner Poem: Eat the Moon 119
- Word Ladders 1 and 2 120
- Mini-Lesson: Grab Bag Buddies 122

References 123
Word Ladder Template 124
Consonant Letter and Cluster Cards 125
Answer Key 128

Meet the Authors

Hello.

I'm David, the poet. My job is to write poems that you can use with your kids. Why verse? Because it rhymes (usually) and has meter (almost always), so its structured language makes it a wonderful classroom tool for learning the poem itself and appreciating the cadence and natural beauty of our language.

Research also tells us that reading as partners further encourages and strengthens children's reading skills. That's why our book takes full advantage of structured language's special qualities by focusing on poems for two or more voices. In this book you'll find 26 original poems, each written for partner reading. I hope you and your students enjoy reading and playing with them as much as I loved writing them for you.

I want to say how happy I am to be partnering with Tim and Mary Jo. In 2009, Tim and I published *Partner Poems for Building Fluency* (Scholastic Teaching Resources), and in 2013 Mary Jo and I wrote *Learning Through Poetry* (Shell Education), a set of five books that featured 96 poems, each inspired by a different phoneme. And now, lucky me, I get to do a book with both of them together!

DAVID L. HARRISON, Litt.D.
Poet Laureate
Drury University

Dear Colleagues:

Mary Jo and I are the professor parts of this endeavor. After years of working with young readers and children who experience difficulty in reading, we have come to the conclusion that poetry is one of the best texts for helping learners improve their reading. Poetry contains certain features that makes it ideal for reading. Poems are usually short, so young children are not overwhelmed by the length of the text. The rhythm and rhyme embedded in poetry makes it easy for children to learn to read and find success in reading. Children who struggle in reading often do not see themselves as successful readers, and this often leads them to believe that they cannot ever become good readers. Poetry counters this notion. In the Reading Clinic at Kent State University, struggling readers learn to read a poem each and every day. It's amazing to see children's faces light up when they go up to their parents to show them that they can read something new each day of the week! Student teachers in central Ohio use poetry in K–8 classrooms to develop a sense of community as children read and laugh together. These student teachers soon discover the power of rhyme and rhythm. They leave their teaching experience ready to use poetry across the curriculum and throughout the day.

Poetry can contain wonderful words that can easily contribute to children's vocabulary development. Moreover, since words in poems often rhyme, poetry lends itself extremely well to children's phonics development (e.g., *If I can read the word* peep *in "Little Bo Peep," I can learn to read* beep, deep, seep, sleep, sweep, steeple, *and many more*). Poems are meant to be read aloud and performed, so they need to be rehearsed or read repeatedly. Repeated reading is one of the best ways to develop reading fluency in children. Poems also contain wonderful and meaningful content that can lead to great discussions that build comprehension. And poems can cross the curriculum. The content of a poem might be just the way to start a science unit on bugs or a social studies unit on mapping.

Reading is also a social activity. To perform a poem, you need an audience. Some poems are written to be recited by more than one reader. We call these "partner poems." David Harrison is one of the very best poets for children around, and he is particularly gifted at writing partner poems.

In light of all this, we happily partnered with David to develop this book for you and your students. Each delightful poem in this collection is meant to be read by two or more readers. Following each poem are Word Ladders, a popular instructional activity that helps children build and learn new words as well as develop their phonics and spelling skills in a fun, gamelike way. Think of all the word games we play as adults. Have you noticed that if you play those games regularly you get better at them? We have a special name for when you get better at something—it's called *learning*! And speaking of learning, each poem also comes with a mini-lesson designed to help children develop proficiency in critical reading, language arts, and curricular competencies.

As you can see, each poem in this book is essentially a complete lesson you can employ with your students, whether you teach a classroom full of children or work as an interventionist with small groups. Children will enjoy reading our poems, playing with words, and developing important reading skills. What could be better than that? Above all, we hope that you and your learners will take great delight in the wonderful words and poems that David Harrison brings to this book.

We wish you and your students lots of fun, plenty of reading, and much progress in building literacy skills.

TIMOTHY RASINSKI, Ph.D.
Professor of Literacy Education
Kent State University

MARY JO FRESCH, Ph.D.
Professor Emerita and Academy Professor
The Ohio State University

What's in This Book

Using lively partner poems along with engaging word ladders and mini-lessons, this comprehensive resource offers a hands-on, ready approach for helping children develop phonics skills, fluency, spelling, word analysis skills, vocabulary, comprehension, and more.

Each partner poem focuses on a particular phonogram, based on the research of Edward Fry (1998) and Wylie and Durrell (1970). Using texts that focus on phonograms provide "early entry into reading for young children" (Menon & Hiebert, 2005, p. 17). In International Literacy Association's 2020 What's Hot in Literacy Report, respondents agreed that "building early literacy skills through a balanced approach that combines both foundational and language comprehension instruction" is critical.

How did we decide on which phonograms to use? Edward Fry discovered that by adding beginning consonants, blends, and digraphs to the 38 most common phonograms found in English, 654 words can be made. Wylie and Durrell similarly identified 37 frequently occurring phonograms that appear in more than 500 primary-level words. The research-based lists of Fry and Wylie and Durrell are highly regarded as providing powerful, independent decoding skills to young readers. Both lists share 26 phonograms in common; Fry suggests 12 more, and Wylie and Durrell found 11 others. Combining these lists provides 49 phonograms and offers a unique approach, not found in any other publications. In our work with young readers, we have found a few additional phonograms that will expand their ability to work across words: -oat, oo, and -ow (diphthong).

We divided the phonograms into two books. One book for Grades K–2 features those phonograms most appropriate for younger learners. This book, for Grades 1–3, highlights the other phonograms (boldfaced in the chart), which provide practice for slightly more experienced readers who are ready to expand their vocabulary and experiences with print.

Of course, the power of these phonograms is not limited to primary-level words. These rimes appear in literally thousands of multisyllabic words; for example, *am = ambulance, camera; ack = acknowledge, backpack; ot = otter, apricot; eed = proceed, seedling.* Providing engaging poems that use these phonograms helps children improve their ability to decode, as well as their reading fluency and comprehension.

ab	ack	ag	**ail**
ain	**ake**	**ale**	am
ame	an	ank	ap
ash	at	**ate**	**aw**
ay	**eat**	ed	**eed**
ell	**est**	ew	**ice**
ick	**ide**	**ight**	ill
im	in	**ine**	ing
ink	ip	it	**oat**
ob	**ock**	**oke**	op
ore	ot	**out**	**ow**
uck	ug	um	ump
unk	y	**oon/ook/ oom**	**ow** (diphthong)

How to Use This Book

This book includes 26 partner poems—one for each featured phonogram—written for two or more readers. The phonograms are listed alphabetically, but you can select any poem that might tie into your ongoing word study or language arts lessons. This makes this resource useful throughout the school year, allowing you to use the poems whenever they naturally fit best in your curriculum.

After you've selected a poem, display it on your board for a whole-class read-aloud and make photocopies for children to practice reading with a partner. Give children plenty of opportunities to read each poem aloud several times. This builds fluency and confidence with the vocabulary. We also recommend having each child keep a notebook of the poems so children can revisit them. The poems can be familiar texts to use during independent reading. You may also reuse a poem when you feel the need to review a particular feature or use it with a different activity.

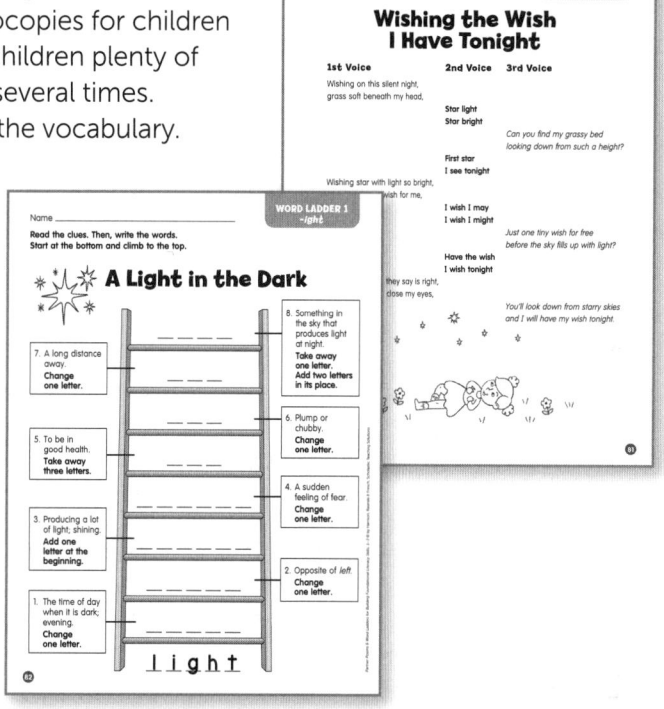

Following each poem are two reproducible Word Ladders that can be used for partner work, in small groups, or with the whole class. Working with Word Ladders is a proven approach for helping children develop their decoding, phonics, spelling, and vocabulary skills in a fun, gamelike way. Word Ladder 1 focuses on phonics and gives children practice on the featured phonogram, while Word Ladder 2 emphasizes vocabulary and may be a bit more challenging.

Word Ladders are easy to implement, and each one takes only about 10 minutes to complete. Simply follow these steps:

1. After children have read, rehearsed, and performed each partner poem, make a copy of the companion Word Ladders for each child. (You may want to start with the simpler Word Ladder 1.)

When a Poem Is "Hard"

Some children may find the poems a bit challenging. We feel that children like challenges. Moreover, research has shown that children can accelerate their reading development when given the opportunity to practice and achieve mastery over challenging texts.

When a poem is challenging for children, you need to provide them with more support and scaffolding. You can do so by displaying an enlarged copy of the poem and reading it aloud while pointing to the words and having children follow along silently. Read the poem with the children chorally multiple times. Have children read while listening to a recorded version of the poem or with a classroom volunteer or with a classmate. And, of course, encourage parents to read the poem with their children multiple times at home, helping them toward the goal of reading (and performing) the poem in class as well as at home for family members.

2. Read aloud the first word at the bottom of the ladder. Invite children to spell the word. Discuss the meaning and any important orthographic (spelling) features of the word.

3. Guide children in working their way up the ladder. For each new word on the ladder, have children read the clues that will help them figure out and spell each new word. Each word comes with three kinds of clues:

   a. the definition of the new word or a sentence in which the word is used in a meaningful context but left out for children to fill in

   b. the kind of spelling changes children need to make to the previous word in order to build the new word (for example, "change the first letter," "take away a letter," "add two letters," or "move the letters around")

   c. the number of letter spaces to make the new word

   Feel free to add your own clues as you go through the words with your students. Direct their attention to specific letters that need to be changed. If a word is difficult, you might have children skip it and move to the next one. Alternatively, you might just want to say the word to children. See if they can write the word from a pronunciation of it. Then be sure to check and discuss its meaning.

4. The final word in each Word Ladder is often related to the first word as well as to the poem children have just read. Children love being challenged to figure out what that last word will be on their own.

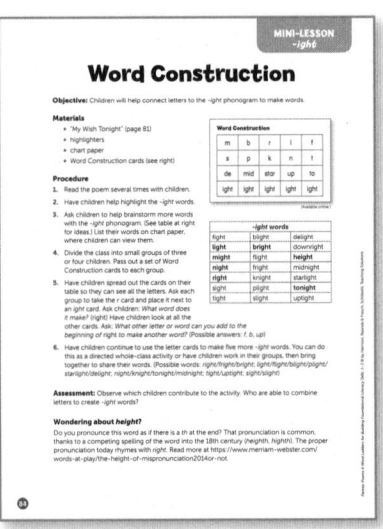

A language arts mini-lesson in reading, writing, or word study also accompanies each poem. A short list of related words containing the phonogram comes with each lesson so you can extend the word study and connect the poem to other content studies. Words used in the poem are boldfaced. The lists are organized by single consonant onsets, consonant blends, and more complex words. In addition, "Wondering About…" examines words used in the poem that "sound" like the phonogram, but are spelled differently. This gives you an opportunity to dive into word histories or puzzle out with children why some words sound similar but have different spellings.

Not Intended for Independent Work

We cannot emphasize enough that the poems, word ladders, and mini-lessons in this book are intended for you, the teacher, to help children become fluent readers and wordsmiths. Children learn best when you guide them as they build fluency with the poems, master the words in the word ladders, and achieve success in the mini-lessons. Some of the words in these activities may not be familiar to children. This is your chance to teach them. When children experience difficulty with a poem, word ladder, or mini-lesson, use this opportunity to provide them with scaffolding that will lead to new word learning. For example, when a word-ladder clue indicates "Change one letter," you can provide support by specifying the letter in the word that needs to be changed. The activities in this book are too valuable to be used as independent seatwork. Rather, we hope you will use these activities to guide children to success and ever-higher levels of reading achievement.

This book (and its companion book for Grades K–2) is designed to let children have fun reading and performing with friends, classmates, teachers, and family members. You can use this resource instructionally on-site, hybrid, or online, with the whole class, in small groups, at home, or in intervention settings to provide effective instruction and practice in reading. Poetry is known to engage striving or reluctant readers because of its use of rhyme, rhythm, and rich but limited-number vocabulary. Poems are also less intimidating to young readers and meant to be rehearsed to improve fluency, confidence, and achieve success.

Ways to Extend Learning

In addition to the suggested lessons, you may wish to extend the experience by having children sort the words into various groups, such as:

- **grammatical categories**—e.g., words that are nouns and words that are not nouns
- **word structure**—e.g., words that have one syllable, two syllables, and three or more syllables; words that contain a long-vowel sound and words that contain a short-vowel sound; words that contain a consonant blend and words that do not
- **word meaning**—e.g., words that express what a person can do or feel and words that do not

This additional analysis through categorization will help children continue to analyze the words more deeply (orthographic mapping) and gain even greater control and understanding over them and related words. Extending examination of the featured phonogram (rime) in a Word Ladder and language arts lesson offers children engaging ways to expand their vocabulary.

Another way to extend children's word study is to choose, along with your students, some of the most interesting words from each Word Ladder activity and put them on display on a class word wall. Encourage children to read and refer to words on the word wall regularly and to use these words in their writing and conversation. And here's a tip about word walls: Put them at a height where they are easily accessible for student use. We often see word walls along the ceiling (where teachers probably have the most room), but this creates a transfer issue for some children as they try to look up and down to copy a word. Putting the words around the room where children can place a paper next to the needed word enables accurate and independent use of the words.

In today's focus on Social and Emotional Learning, we can think of no better vehicle for fostering community than using poetry for two or more voices. Such poems encourage working with others, which "increases student interest in learning, improves student behavior, prevents and reduces bullying, and improves school climate" (Bridgeland & Bruce, 2013). Regardless of how you are delivering instruction, we hope you and your children will have fun with these phonograms!

> **Bonus Online Materials:** To access printable templates and additional resources for this book, go to **www.scholastic.com/partnerpoemswordladders** and enter your email address and access code: **SC734191**.

Jail Break!

1st Voice

I just heard the news about Gail!

Gail the Snail broke out of jail!

They just can't keep her in the pen.
I got the news in a long email.

Gail.
She said no matter how they tried,
they'd never keep her cooped inside.

Without a trail.

Turns out Gail is one smart snail.
She used her boyfriend, Bob the Quail.
Bob flew down, she grabbed his tail,
and off they went on a getaway sail.

They'll never catch Bob Quail and Gail.

2nd Voice

News about Gail?
Gail the Snail?

Gail broke out of jail again?

Who would send an email?

And now she's gone?

How could a snail not leave a trail?

All over town the sirens wail.

Name _____

WORD LADDER 1
-ail

**Read the clues. Then, write the words.
Start at the bottom and climb to the top.**

Go, Snail, Go!

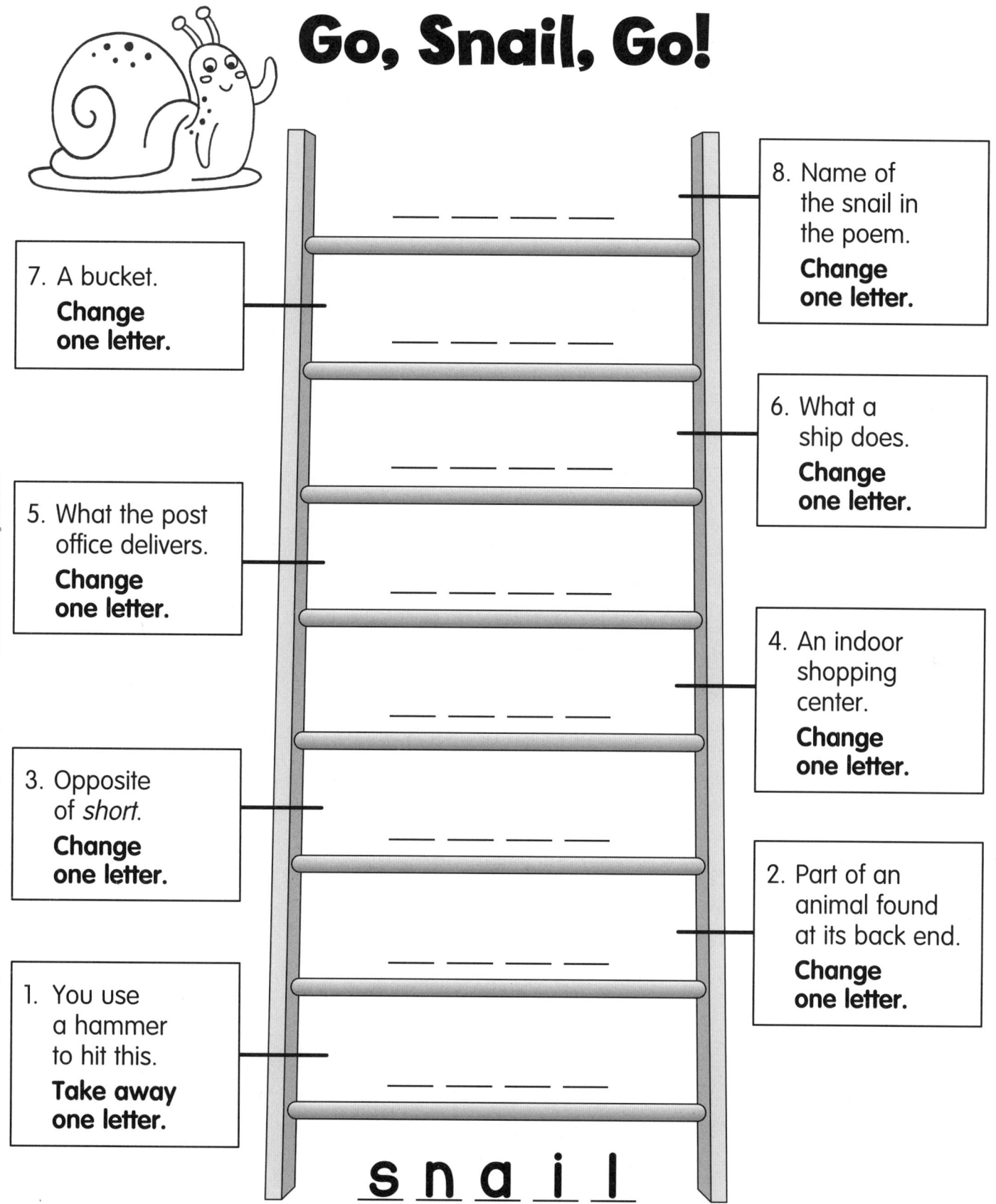

8. Name of the snail in the poem. **Change one letter.**

7. A bucket. **Change one letter.**

6. What a ship does. **Change one letter.**

5. What the post office delivers. **Change one letter.**

4. An indoor shopping center. **Change one letter.**

3. Opposite of *short*. **Change one letter.**

2. Part of an animal found at its back end. **Change one letter.**

1. You use a hammer to hit this. **Take away one letter.**

s n a i l

WORD LADDER 2
-ail

Name _____

Read the clues. Then, write the words.
Start at the bottom and climb to the top.

Let's Take the Train!

9. A street. When combined with the first word, what trains ride on.
Change one letter.

8. An animal that looks like a frog.
Add one letter.

7. A very small amount of something.
Change the first letter.

6. Angry.
Take away one letter.

5. A woman who cleans rooms in a hotel.
Change one letter.

4. Most important; many streets have this name.
Change one letter.

3. Letters delivered by a postal worker.
Take away two letters. Add one letter in their place.

2. A path or track to walk on, like in the woods.
Change two letters.

1. Type of bird from the poem.
Take away one letter. Add two letters in its place.

r a i l

MINI-LESSON
-ail

Write a Riddle

Objective: Children will write a riddle in which the answer is an *-ail* word.

Materials
- "Jail Break!" (page 12)
- highlighters
- chart paper
- paper and pencil (or tablets or computers)

Procedure
1. Read the poem several times with children.
2. Have children highlight the *-ail* words in the poem.
3. Ask children: *What other words do you know that end with* -ail? List their words on chart paper, where children can view them.
4. Have children choose one of the highlighted or listed words to write a riddle about. Provide an example: "I use this to carry sand at the beach." (*Pail*) Then have children write their own riddles.
5. Take time to have children read their riddles aloud, inviting classmates to guess the answer.

Assessment: Are children able to show they know the meaning of the chosen word by the riddles they wrote? You might want to have small groups work together to write riddles for more complex words so you can further assess their vocabulary knowledge.

-ail words		
fail	frail	ailment
Gail	**quail**	available
hail	**snail**	bailiff
jail	**trail**	detail
mail		**email**
nail		entail
pail		failure
rail		prevail
sail		retail
tail		tailor
wail		

The Muddy Drain Stain

1st Voice

There once was a girl named Elaine
who seldom was heard to complain,

And left her a muddy drain stain.

But I scour in vain
and make little gain.

2nd Voice

But one day the rain
washed mud down her drain

"This stain," sighed Elaine, "is a pain.
I scrub and I scrape and I strain.

In the end, all I have is a sprain."

Name _____

WORD LADDER 1
-ain

**Read the clues. Then, write the words.
Start at the bottom and climb to the top.**

Ouch, My Ankle!

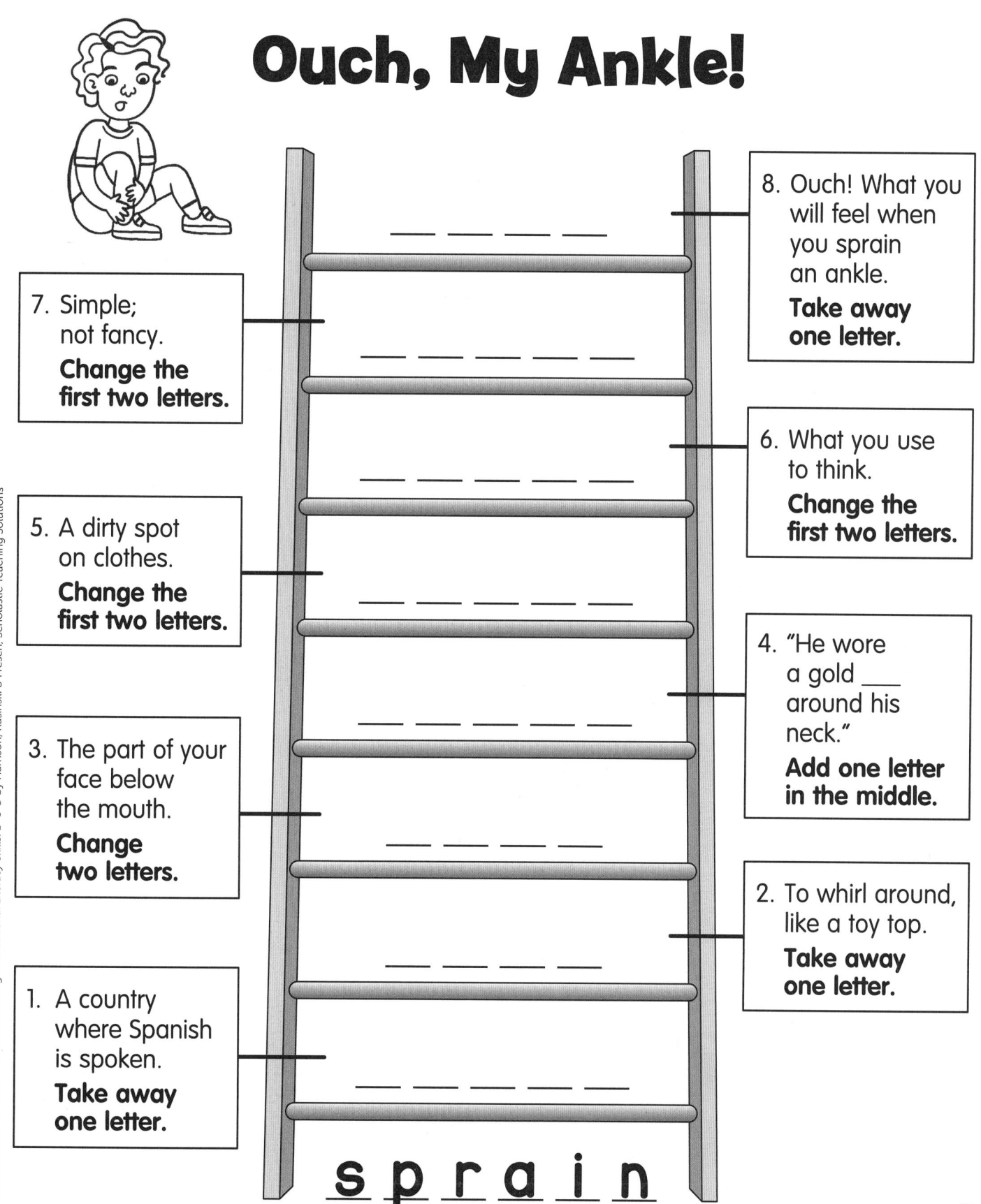

8. Ouch! What you will feel when you sprain an ankle. **Take away one letter.**

7. Simple; not fancy. **Change the first two letters.**

6. What you use to think. **Change the first two letters.**

5. A dirty spot on clothes. **Change the first two letters.**

4. "He wore a gold ___ around his neck." **Add one letter in the middle.**

3. The part of your face below the mouth. **Change two letters.**

2. To whirl around, like a toy top. **Take away one letter.**

1. A country where Spanish is spoken. **Take away one letter.**

s p r a i n

WORD LADDER 2
-ain

Name _____

Read the clues. Then, write the words.
Start at the bottom and climb to the top.

No Grumbling

9. What Elaine seldom did. **Add three letters at the beginning.**

8. A large area of flat land; sounds like *plane*. **Add one letter.**

7. To figure out ahead of time how to do something. **Take away one letter.**

6. A vehicle that flies through the air. **Add one letter.**

5. A sheet of glass in a window; sounds like *pain*. **Add one letter.**

4. Something used for frying food. **Change one letter.**

3. An adult male. **Take away one letter.**

2. Long hair on the back of a horse. **Change one letter.**

1. A narrow street. **Take away two letters.**

E l a i n e

MINI-LESSON
-ain

Make a Word Search

Objective: Children will make a word search using the *-ain* words in the poem.

Materials

- "The Muddy Drain Stain" (page 16)
- highlighters
- pencils
- graph/grid paper or create a 10-by-12 grid on plain paper (see right)

Procedure

1. Invite children to read the poem several times.

2. Have children highlight the *-ain* words in the poem. Tell them that they will create a word search using the *-ain* words from the poem.

3. Distribute graph paper or copies of the 10-by-12 grid. Have children write one of the longer words (such as *complain*) across the middle, putting one letter per square. On the board, model how to write the letters in the grid.

4. Next, tell children to write as many of the *-ain* words as they can in the remainder of the grid. Tell them the words can share letters. Provide an example on the board, as shown above.

5. When children have put in all their chosen *-ain* words, have them randomly fill letters into any blank squares.

6. Have children exchange word searches. Then challenge them to look for and highlight the words they see from the poem.

7. To extend the word learning, have children brainstorm and make a list of other *-ain* words. They could then make a second word search using all the words or just the new, brainstormed words.

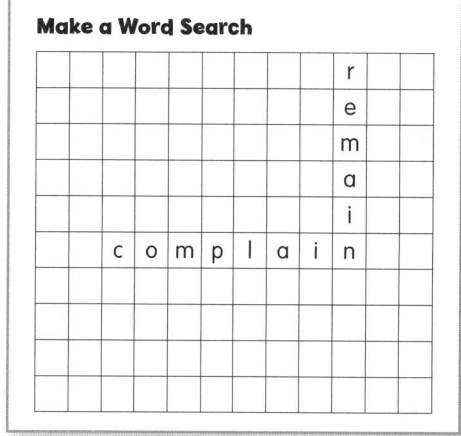
(Available online.)

-ain words		
gain	brain	**complain**
lain	chain	contain
main	**drain**	detain
pain	faint	Elaine
rain	grain	explain
vain	paint	obtain
	plain	ordain
	slain	painful
	Spain	remain
	sprain	retain
	stain	
	strain	
	train	

Assessment: Do children correctly transfer the correct spelling of the *-ain* words to create the word search? Are they able to plan ahead to include several of the poem words? Who contributed to create the list of more complex *-ain* words? This indicates their ability to hear the sound and generalize it to other vocabulary words they know.

Saved by the Snake

PARTNER POEM *-ake*

1st Voice (Blake)	**2nd Voice (Jake)**

One evening
we went camping
by a lake.

                    Next morning,
                    we decided
                    we would make

Something to eat
to help us
get awake.

                    Blake made
                    a pancake.
                    Big mistake.

A bear smelled it
clear across
the lake.

(continued)

PARTNER POEM
-ake

1st Voice (Blake)   **2nd Voice (Jake)**

                               There's nothing
                               like a bear
                               to make you shake.

Jake and I both
began
to quake.

                               We thought fast!
                               How,
                               for goodness' sake,

Do you stop a bear,
swimming
across a lake?

                               Worried
                               that our pancake
                               was at stake,

We threw
the only thing we had—
a snake.

                               There in the lake
                               the bear
                               put on the brake,

Turned around
and left
a bear-sized wake.

                               So glad
                               he didn't know

Our snake
was fake.

WORD LADDER 1
-ake

Name _____

Read the clues. Then, write the words.
Start at the bottom and climb to the top.

Is It Real?

9. Something that is not what it seems.
Change one letter.

8. Where your eyes, nose, and mouth are located.
Change one letter.

7. A type of fancy cloth.
Change one letter.

6. A body of water larger than a pond.
Change one letter.

5. To enjoy something.
Change one letter.

4. A shortened name for a bicycle.
Change one letter.

3. What you do with dough to turn it into bread.
Change one letter.

2. "I have to ___ care of my little brother today."
Take away one letter.

1. A pointed stick that can be pushed into the ground.
Change one letter.

s n a k e

WORD LADDER 2
-ake

Name _____

Read the clues. Then, write the words. Start at the bottom and climb to the top.

Something Sweet

9. What a raindrop may turn into when it is cold. **Add four letters at the beginning.**

8. A small piece of snow or corn cereal. **Change one letter.**

7. The light given off by a fire. **Add one letter at the beginning.**

6. Having a hurt leg, making it hard to walk. **Change one letter.**

5. A body of water smaller than an ocean. **Change one letter.**

4. To build or create something. **Take away three letters.**

3. An error or something wrong. **Add three letters at the beginning.**

2. Opposite of *give*. **Change one letter.**

1. A baked dessert usually made for birthdays. **Take away three letters.**

c u p c a k e

MINI-LESSON
-ake

Word Webs

Objective: Children will create webs of related *-ake* words.

Materials
- "Saved by the Snake" (page 20)
- highlighters
- paper and pencil

Procedure

1. Invite children to read the poem several times.

2. Have children highlight the *-ake* words in the poem.

3. Take one of the words (for example, *cake*) and write it in the center of a web. Ask children: *Can you think of other words that have* cake *in them?* You may need to give clues to help children come up with related words (for example, "You pour syrup on this breakfast food").

4. Together as a class, discuss other related words and add them to the web.

Other possible webs include: **make**—*makeup, remake, coffeemaker, shoemaker, makeover;* **sake**—*forsake, namesake, keepsake;* **quake**—*quaked, Quakers, earthquake;* **flake**—*snowflake, cornflake;* **shake**—*handshake, milkshake, unshaken, shaker.*

Assessment: Are some children able to add to the web without the help of your clues? Once you give clues, does that spark a memory of a related word?

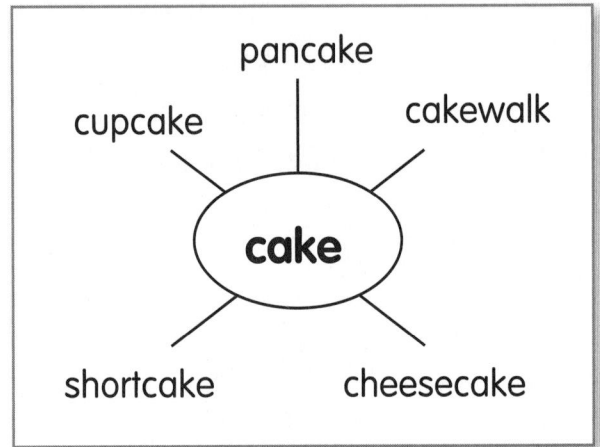

-ake words		
bake	**Blake**	awake
cake	**brake**	bakery
fake	drake	cupcake
Jake	flake	forsake
lake	quake	handshake
make	**shake**	**mistake**
rake	snake	**pancake**
sake	**stake**	shaker
take		snowflake
wake		

PARTNER POEM
-ale

Don't Eat That!

1st Voice (Mama) **2nd Voice (Child)**

Darling, try
a little kale.
It's good for you.

                                    I hate kale.
                                    It tastes bad.
                                    Yuck! Poo!

Dear, it's rich
in vitamins
that children need.

                                    I'd rather chew
                                    a bale of
                                    dandelion weed.

It only takes
a bite of kale
to keep you hale.

                                    I'd rather eat
                                    a Clydesdale
                                    or a blue whale.

Sweetie, taste
this kale before
it goes stale.

                                    Why do you keep
                                    pushing me
                                    to eat kale?

Because I bought
a ton of kale.
It was on sale.

WORD LADDER 1
-ale

Name _____

Read the clues. Then, write the words.
Start at the bottom and climb to the top.

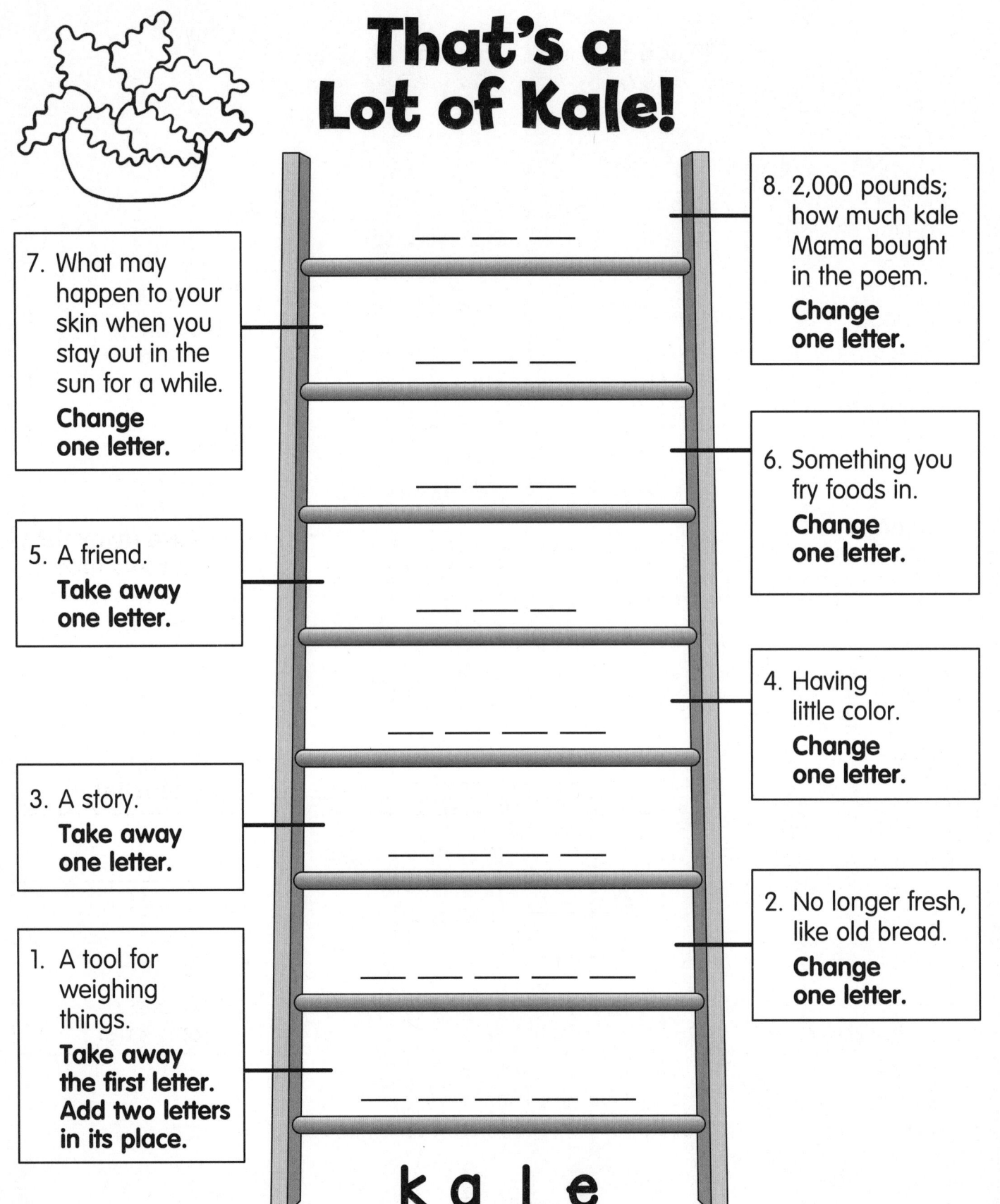

That's a Lot of Kale!

8. 2,000 pounds; how much kale Mama bought in the poem. **Change one letter.**

7. What may happen to your skin when you stay out in the sun for a while. **Change one letter.**

6. Something you fry foods in. **Change one letter.**

5. A friend. **Take away one letter.**

4. Having little color. **Change one letter.**

3. A story. **Take away one letter.**

2. No longer fresh, like old bread. **Change one letter.**

1. A tool for weighing things. **Take away the first letter. Add two letters in its place.**

k a l e

WORD LADDER 2
-ale

Name _____

Read the clues. Then, write the words.
Start at the bottom and climb to the top.

Tell Me a Story

9. A story. Combined with the first word, a type of story passed down over the years. **Change one letter.**

8. A valley. **Change one letter.**

7. A particular month, day, or year. **Change one letter.**

6. A partner or buddy. **Take away the first two letters. Then, change one letter.**

5. A girl or woman. **Add two letters at the beginning.**

4. A boy or man. **Change one letter.**

3. A furry animal that lives mostly underground. **Change one letter.**

2. Something that grows on rotten food. **Change one letter.**

1. To bend clothing or paper. **Change one letter.**

f o l k

MINI-LESSON
-ale

Homophone Challenge

Objective: Children will work with buddies to find homophone partners of poem *-ale* words.

Materials
- "Don't Eat That!" (page 25)
- highlighters
- paper and pencil

Procedure

1. Invite children to read the poem several times.
2. Have them highlight words with *-ale* in the poem.
3. On the board, list the following *-ale* words: *bale, hale, male, pale, sale, tale, vale, whale.*
4. Ask children: *What do we call words that sound the same but have different meanings or spellings from each other? For example,* new *and* knew. (Homophones) Tell children that the words on the board have homophones—words that sound the same but are spelled differently.
5. Partner up children and give each pair paper and pencil. Have partners work together to write the other spelling for each word on the board.
6. When they are done, have children share their spellings with the class. (Answers: *bail, hail, mail, pail, sail, tail, vail, wail*)
7. Ask: *What do you notice about the homophones?* (All are spelled with the *-ail* phonogram.) Share with children that words that sound the same but are spelled differently came to English from different origins. (For example, *mail* has Germanic roots, while *male* has French roots.)

-ale words		
bale	scale	**Clydesdale**
dale	shale	exhale
gale	**stale**	fairytale
hale	**whale**	female
kale		folktale
male		
pale		
sale		
tale		
vale		
yale		

Note: You may want to consult a website such as https://www.etymonline.com to discover other word origins.

Assessment: Are children able to write the homophone pairs? Do they notice the *-ail* common spelling?

The Night the Great Goat Came

PARTNER POEM
-ame

| **1st Voice** | **All Together** | **2nd Voice** |

One moonlit night
Great Goat came.
His beard was long
and red as flame.
We took one look
and knew he had
  no shame.

        His beard was red.
        He had no shame.

                He smiled and said,
                "I'm not to blame.
                Making trouble
                is my game.
                Everywhere I go
                is just the same."

        His beard was red.
        He had no shame.
        Making trouble
        was his game.

Sure enough
the troubles came,
with Great Goat saying,
"I'm not to blame."
Then he'd smile
to show he had
  no shame.

(continued)

PARTNER POEM
-ame

1st Voice   **All Together**   **2nd Voice**

All Together:
His beard was red.
He had no shame.
Making trouble
was his game.
Trouble started
when he came.

2nd Voice:
*He left at last,
the way he came—
one moonlit night,
red beard aflame.
Without a sound
Great Goat went away.*

1st Voice:
Where he went,
no one could say.
We jumped and clapped
and yelled, "Hooray!"
Not a soul
has seen him to this day.

2nd Voice:
*No one ever
took the blame.*

1st Voice:
We never learned
just what became

All Together:
Of Great Goat
whom none could tame,
whose beard was long
and red as flame,
and making trouble
was his game,
but never, never
took the blame—
The Great Goat
who had no sense
  of shame.

WORD LADDER 1
-ame

Name _____

Read the clues. Then, write the words.
Start at the bottom and climb to the top.

Who's to Blame?

7. Two things that are exactly alike are the ___.
Take away the last letter. Add two letters in its place.

8. Great Goat had none of this.
Add one letter.

6. To speak.
Change one letter.

5. The month after April.
Change one letter.

4. It's 24 hours long.
Change one letter.

3. Another word for *no*.
Take away the last two letters. Add one letter in their place.

2. What a person is called.
Change one letter.

1. Having a hurt leg that makes walking hard.
Take away one letter.

b l a m e

WORD LADDER 2
-ame

Name _____

Read the clues. Then, write the words.
Start at the bottom and climb to the top.

Greatest of All Time

8. Something more important than normal; the ___ Goat from the story.
Take away one letter. Add two letters in its place.

7. Food that comes from an animal, such as a cow or pig.
Move the letters around.

6. A close friend or partner.
Move the letters around.

5. A gentle animal that is not afraid of people.
Change one letter.

4. Having a hard time walking.
Take away one letter.

3. The glowing part of a fire.
Take away one letter. Add two letters in its place.

2. Level; not hilly or bumpy.
Take away one letter.

1. To stay on the surface of water, like a boat.
Take away one letter. Add two letters in its place.

g o a t

MINI-LESSON
-ame

Same as Similes

Objective: Children will write similes.

Materials
- "The Night the Great Goat Came" (page 29)
- highlighters
- paper and pencil

Procedure

1. Invite children to read the poem several times.
2. Have them highlight the *-ame* words in the poem.
3. Ask children: *What words were used to describe Goat's beard?* (Red as flame) Explain that descriptions that use the words *like* or *as* to compare two things are called *similes*. Give the following examples and discuss their meanings with children.
    - The new teacher was as cold as ice.
    - My aunt is as sweet as sugar.
    - My dad is as strong as an ox.
4. List the following simile starters on the board.

Cold as . . .	Happy as . . .
Jumpy as . . .	Slippery as . . .
Bright as . . .	Tall as . . .
Funny as . . .	Slow as . . .

5. Partner up children and give each pair paper and pencil. Have partners work together to complete the similes on the board.
6. Invite children to share their favorite similes. Then post them on the wall for all to read in their free time.

Assessment: Listen as children work together to come up with possible similes. Their responses will give insights into their vocabulary knowledge.

-ame words		
came	**blame**	**aflame**
dame	**flame**	**became**
fame	frame	
game	**shame**	
lame		
name		
same		
tame		

The Odd Case of the Lash Hash

1st Voice

Yesterday my sister said,
"I think I'll make some hash."

You might not like my sister's hash.
She throws in stuff slapdash.

Yesterday she lost a lash
that landed with a splash.

The bowl fell with a loud crash
that sent her hash kersplash!

She made another bowl of hash
and ate without the lash.

2nd Voice

Oooh, that sounds wonderful!
I love a yummy hash.

Forgive me if I sound too brash,
I might not like her hash.

Wow! What a heavy lash
to make a hash go splash!

Oh my goodness! Did it smash?
Did Sister find her lash?

Name _____

WORD LADDER 1
-ash

**Read the clues. Then, write the words.
Start at the bottom and climb to the top.**

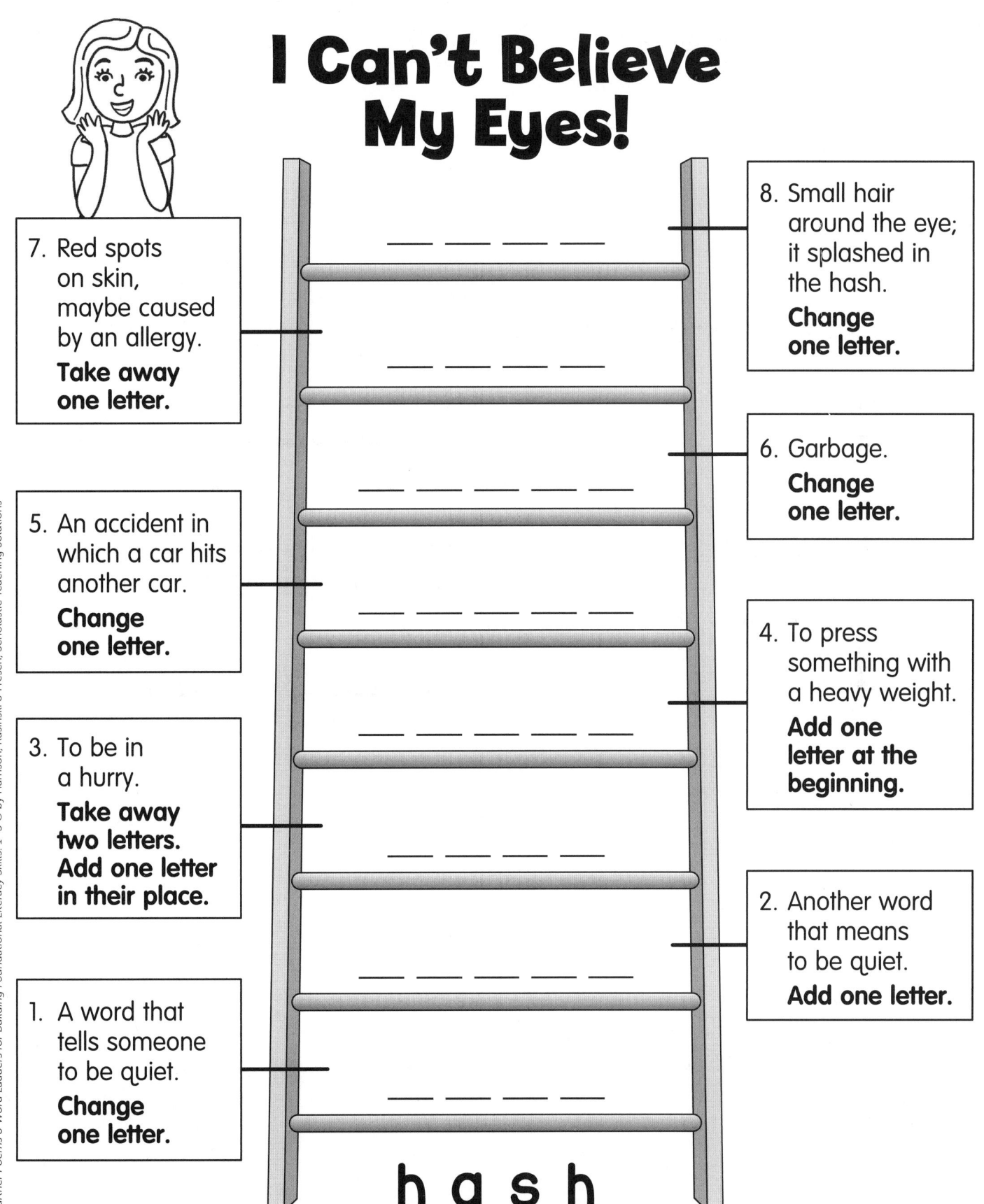

I Can't Believe My Eyes!

8. Small hair around the eye; it splashed in the hash. **Change one letter.**

7. Red spots on skin, maybe caused by an allergy. **Take away one letter.**

6. Garbage. **Change one letter.**

5. An accident in which a car hits another car. **Change one letter.**

4. To press something with a heavy weight. **Add one letter at the beginning.**

3. To be in a hurry. **Take away two letters. Add one letter in their place.**

2. Another word that means to be quiet. **Add one letter.**

1. A word that tells someone to be quiet. **Change one letter.**

h a s h

WORD LADDER 2
-ash

Name _____

Read the clues. Then, write the words.
Start at the bottom and climb to the top.

In a Hurry

9. A short running race. Combined with the first word, it means to do something in a hurry. **Change one letter.**

8. To crush food into something soft, like potatoes. **Change one letter.**

7. A thick, soft glob of something, such as oatmeal. **Change one letter.**

6. A lot or plenty of something. **Take away one letter.**

5. To chew or eat food. **Change one letter.**

4. Meal served around noon. **Take away two letters. Add three letters in their place.**

3. A bump that forms after being hit by a ball. **Change one letter.**

2. A light someone might have on a desk. **Add one letter.**

1. A child sometimes sits on her parent's ___. **Take away one letter.**

s l a p

-ash Crossword

MINI-LESSON
-ash

Objective: Children will work in small groups to solve a crossword puzzle that uses words from the poem.

Materials
- "The Odd Case of the Lash Hash" (page 34)
- highlighters
- -ash Crossword* (see right)

* You may choose to project the crossword on the board for the class to solve together or photocopy for individuals or partners.

Procedure
1. Invite children to read the poem several times.
2. Have children help highlight the *-ash* words in the poem.
3. Display the crossword puzzle on the board and/or distribute copies to children. Together, have children read the Across clue #2 and look for the *-ash* word in the poem that defines it. (For example: Sound of a liquid falling—*splash*.)
4. Have children complete the rest of the crossword as a group or with a partner. Remind them to refer to the poem to find the words.

Crossword Clues (and Answers)
Across

2. Sound of a liquid falling (*splash*)

4. To run into something (*crash*)

5. A type of meal (*hash*)

7. Noise of a liquid spilling (*kersplash*)

Down

1. Hair on the eyelid (*lash*)

2. To break into pieces (*smash*)

3. To do something in a hurry (*slapdash*)

6. To be rude (*brash*)

Crossword

(Available online.)

-ash words		
bash	**brash**	balderdash
cash	clash	eyelash
dash	**crash**	**kersplash**
flash	slash	rehash
gash	**smash**	**slapdash**
hash	**splash**	whiplash
lash	stash	
mash	trash	
rash		
sash		

Assessment: Circulate as children work together on the crossword, listening for their strategies to figure out the words.

37

Nate and Kate's Date

1st Voice

We love our cow.
Her name is Nate.

2nd Voice

You can't call
a cow Nate.
She's a girl.
Call her Kate.

Can't call her Kate.
We have a bull.
His name is Kate.

A bull called Kate?
A cow named Nate?

At any rate,
one day Nate
opened the gate.

What about Kate?

Oh, Kate came, too.
Nate's Kate's mate.
It was a date.

(continued)

PARTNER POEM -ate

1st Voice	**2nd Voice**
	Let me see
	if I have this straight.
	Kate, the bull,
	and Nate, the cow,
	went on a date,
	opened the gate,
	and got out somehow.
Close, but Kate	
was running late.	
He didn't see	
the gate grate.	
	What?
The grate	
below the gate,	
there to keep in	
Kate and Nate.	
Kate's nose ring	
got stuck in the grate.	
	Okay, okay.
	Kate, the bull,
	and Nate, the cow,
	went on a date,
	opened the gate.
	Kate was late
	and got stuck
	in the grate.
Right. I hate	
to relate Kate's fate,	
but that gate grate	
ruined their date.	

WORD LADDER 1
-ate

Name _____

Read the clues. Then, write the words.
Start at the bottom and climb to the top.

Moo-ve It!

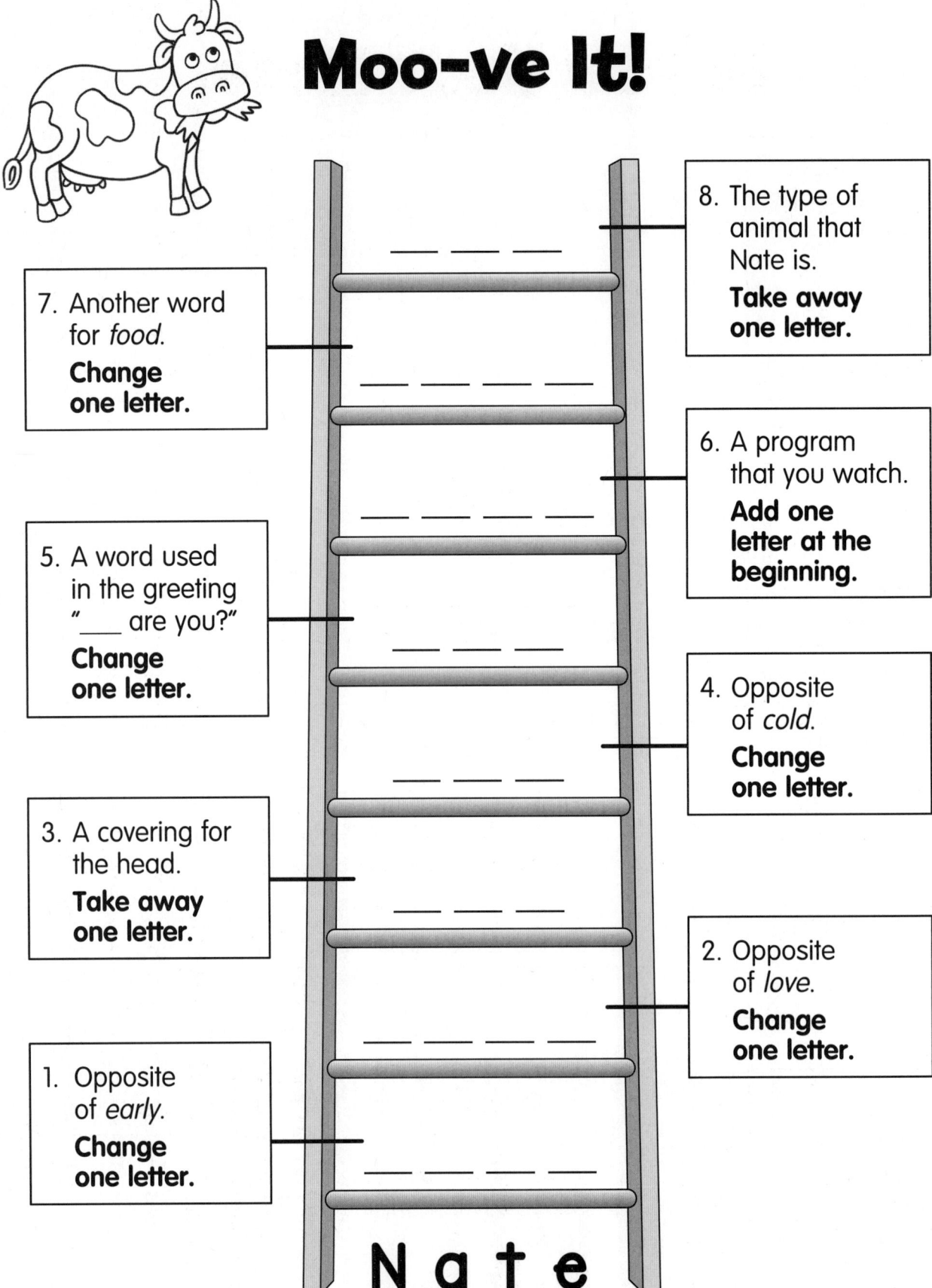

8. The type of animal that Nate is. **Take away one letter.**

7. Another word for *food*. **Change one letter.**

6. A program that you watch. **Add one letter at the beginning.**

5. A word used in the greeting "___ are you?" **Change one letter.**

4. Opposite of *cold*. **Change one letter.**

3. A covering for the head. **Take away one letter.**

2. Opposite of *love*. **Change one letter.**

1. Opposite of *early*. **Change one letter.**

N a t e

WORD LADDER 2
-ate

Name _____

Read the clues. Then, write the words.
Start at the bottom and climb to the top.

Follow Your Nose

9. Crossed metal bars that cover an opening; where Kate's nose ring got stuck. **Add one letter.**

8. An opening in a fence that can open and close. **Change one letter.**

7. To look at someone or something steadily. **Change one letter.**

6. A puzzle with different paths through which you have to find a way out. **Change one letter.**

5. Something that was built has been ___. **Add one letter.**

4. To be very angry. **Change one letter.**

3. An adult male. **Change one letter.**

2. More than one man. **Change one letter.**

1. A tool for writing with ink. **Take away one letter.**

o p e n

MINI-LESSON
-ate

Hop Along

Objective: Children will correctly read words on paper "stepping stones."

Materials
- "Nate and Kate's Date" (page 38)
- highlighters
- 24 4-by-6-inch blank index cards*
- number cube or die

* Alternatively, you can cut paper the shape of stones to add visual fun!

Procedure

1. Invite children to read the poem together several times.
2. Ask children to help you highlight the *-ate* words in the poem.
3. Divide the class into two teams. Distribute 12 blank "stepping stones" (index cards) to each team. Ask one child from each team to write *gate* on an index card. Continue reading each highlighted word aloud until the teams have created two sets of the words.
4. Ask children: *Can you think of any other -ate words?* If necessary, give a hint, such as: *This -ate word is what I put food on.* (Plate) Have teams add these words to their sets of cards until each team has a total of 12 cards.
5. Lay each team's 12 cards out in a line. (You can mix the order for each team.)
6. Roll the die for Team 1 to get the number of "stones" the first player must "hop" on. The player must read aloud each word she steps on. Allow teammates to help if the player gets stuck with a word.
7. Repeat step 6 for Team 2.
8. When the first player reaches the last stone, the next player in the team takes a turn.
9. Continue until all children have had a turn to hop on the "stones." The team that has all players reach the last word first wins.

-ate words		
ate	crate	debate
date	**grate**	playmate
fate	plate	**relate**
gate	skate	roommate
hate	slate	schoolmate
Kate	state	teammate
late		
mate		
Nate		
rate		

Note: You can strategically line up children on each time, placing the ones who might need more support toward the end of the line so they can hear the words read aloud several times.

Assessment: Which children are able to read the words independently and which ones need assistance? Which children could think of other *-ate* words to add to the game?

The Oddest Crow

PARTNER POEM -aw

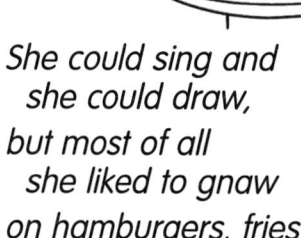

1st Voice	All Together	2nd Voice
The oddest crow I ever saw lived on a lake in Arkansas.		
	Caw! Caw! Caw!	
		She could sing and she could draw, but most of all she liked to gnaw on hamburgers, fries, and slaw.
	Caw! Caw! Caw!	
She'd open wide and stuff her jaw		
		With hamburgers, fries, and slaw,
Admire herself and sing, "Ha-ha, I'm the oddest crow in Arkansas!"		
		And off she'd go with a "Caw, caw!"
	Caw! Caw! Caw!	
She'd grab a french fry by a claw, Dip it in ketchup, then she'd draw		
		A big old burger and a bucket of slaw ... The oddest crow in Arkansas.
	Caw! Caw! Caw! Caw!	
Caw!		Caw!
	Caw!	

Name _____

WORD LADDER 1
-aw

**Read the clues. Then, write the words.
Start at the bottom and climb to the top.**

Bye, Black Bird

8. Sound made by a crow.
   Change one letter.

7. Bones in the lower part of your face that hold your teeth.
   Change one letter.

6. A rule made by the government.
   Change one letter.

5. Opposite of *high*.
   Change one letter.

4. A loud noise, as when something is hit.
   Change one letter.

3. The foot of a dog or cat.
   Change one letter.

2. Uncooked, as in food.
   Change one letter.

1. To move a boat through water with oars.
   Take away one letter.

c r o w

Name _____

WORD LADDER 2
-aw

Read the clues. Then, write the words.
Start at the bottom and climb to the top.

With Fries on the Side

7. Part of the sound a donkey makes: hee-___.
Take away two letters. Add one letter in their place.

5. Meat that is not cooked is ___.
Change one letter.

3. To move quickly with your legs.
Change one letter.

1. What logs in a fire will do.
Take away the last three letters. Add one letter in their place.

8. A type of meat. Combined with the first word, a type of sandwich.
Change one letter.

6. To make a picture with a pencil or pen.
Add one letter.

4. "Yesterday I ___ in a race."
Change one letter.

2. Bread you put a burger on.
Take away one letter.

b u r g e r

45

MINI-LESSON
-aw

Draw a Word

Objective: Children will play a card game that requires reading *-aw* words.

Materials

- "The Oddest Crow" (page 43)
- highlighters
- 28 blank index cards (for each small group of 4 or 5 children)

Procedure

1. For each small group of children, write each of the following *-aw* words on four index cards: *caw, saw, draw, gnaw, slaw, jaw, claw*. You'll end up with 28 cards for each group.

2. Invite children to read the poem together several times.

3. Ask children to help you highlight the *-aw* words in the poem.

4. Divide the class into groups of four or five children. Shuffle the cards and stack them facedown between the players.

5. To play, each player draws four cards from the stack. Players look at their cards. If they have two cards with matching words, they read the word aloud and lay the matching cards in front of them.

6. The first player draws a card from the stack. He decides whether to keep the card or discard it.

7. The next player may take the discarded word card or draw a new card from the stack. Whenever players make a pair of the same word, they must read the word aloud and then lay the matching cards in front of them.

8. Play continues until no more matches can be made. The player with the most matches wins. (If the stack runs out of cards before the game ends, have players shuffle the discard pile and stack the cards facedown to use again.)

-aw words		
caw	**claw**	bylaw
haw	craw	coleslaw
jaw	**draw**	hacksaw
law	flaw	jigsaw
paw	**gnaw**	oversaw
raw	**slaw**	withdraw
saw	straw	
	thaw	

Assessment: Listen for correct identification as children read their word pairs.

Starving in the Back Seat

1st Voice

Mile after mile with nothing to eat,
I'm starving to death in the back seat.

There's nothing but nothing but acres
  of wheat,
and all I can think of is something to eat.

I dream of bananas and crackers and meat
and anything, anything, something to eat.

Reading is dandy, the story is neat,
but I cannot stop wishing for some little treat.

My parents don't get it, I try to explain,
something to eat is the thing on my brain.

But mile after mile I sigh in defeat,
starving to death in the back seat.

2nd Voice

"If you look out the window," my parents
  repeat,
"it will help you stop thinking of something
  to eat."

"Fluff up your pillow," my parents repeat.
"A nap will pass time and you won't need
  to eat."

"Read a good book," my parents repeat.
"Reading will help you stop wanting to eat."

"Draw us some pictures," my parents
  repeat.
"They'll help take your mind off
  something to eat."

Over and over my parents repeat
something to do so I won't want to eat.

WORD LADDER 1
-eat

Name _____

Read the clues. Then, write the words.
Start at the bottom and climb to the top.

Are We There Yet?

1. A stand on which to place things, such as a coat ___.
   Change one letter.

2. A contest of speed, like running.
   Change one letter.

3. In a deck of cards, it's the same as "one."
   Take away one letter.

4. To have eaten before. "Yesterday I ___ a taco."
   Change one letter.

5. What we do with food.
   Move around the letters.

6. A special, delicious food. Also, "trick or ___!"
   Add two letters at the beginning.

7. Food that comes from animals.
   Take away two letters. Add one letter in their place.

8. Combined with the first word, the part of the car where children usually sit.
   Change one letter.

b a c k

48

WORD LADDER 2
-eat

Name _____

Read the clues. Then, write the words. Start at the bottom and climb to the top.

Nap Time

9. Something you lay your head on in bed. **Add two letters.**

8. A farm tool pulled by a tractor to turn over soil. **Change one letter.**

7. The story line in a book. **Take away the first letter. Add two letters in its place.**

6. Opposite of *cold*. **Take away the two vowels. Add one vowel in their place.**

5. To make something hot. **Take away one letter.**

4. To act in a dishonest way **Take away the first letter. Add two letters in its place.**

3. Food that comes from an animal, such as a cow or pig. **Add one letter.**

2. A small piece of cloth that covers the floor. **Change one letter.**

1. A chart used to help you get from one place to another. **Change one letter.**

n a p

MINI-LESSON -eat

Spoons for -eats

Objective: Children will create -eat words.

Materials (for each small group)
- "Starving in the Back Seat" (page 47)
- highlighters
- 6 plastic spoons and permanent marker (or 6 copies of paper spoons and pencil; see right)
- index card with -eat written on it

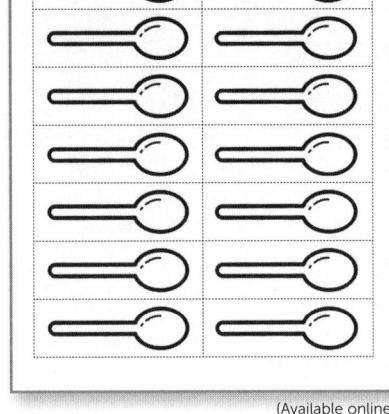

(Available online.)

Procedure
1. Invite children to read the poem several times.
2. Ask them to help you highlight the -eat words.
3. Divide the class into small groups. Give each group six blank spoons and an -eat card.
4. Ask each group to take one spoon and write *m* on it. Have them put the spoon in front of -eat. Ask: *What word do you have?* (meat)

5. Using the poem for reference, have children find five more -eat words and write the beginning letters on the spoons. They may also make other -eat words they know. You may also want to suggest some additional words. For example, "If I put *b* on a spoon, what word do I have?" (beat)
6. After each group has used all six spoons, have them share their words with the class.
7. Place these at a workstation for children to revisit during work time.

Assessment: Are children able to create -eat words? Do they make words that were not in the poem?

-eat words		
beat	bleat	**defeat**
eat	cheat	heartbeat
feat	pleat	preheat
heat	**treat**	offbeat
meat	**wheat**	reheat
neat		**repeat**
seat		

Never Feed a Centipede

1st Voice

Don't ask me why,
but I agreed
to feed my brother's
centipede.

I tried a
dandelion weed,
but with the weed
I did not succeed.

No luck with the weed.
It didn't seem
to see the need.

2nd Voice

That was very
kind indeed.
What do you feed
a centipede?

No luck with the weed?

(continued)

PARTNER POEM -eed

1st Voice	2nd Voice
	Perhaps your brother's centipede wanted seed instead of weed.
It turned down seed and weed and reed.	
	What a picky centipede. Your brother's pet is an odd breed.
I let it go. When it was freed, it crawled away at top speed.	
	Did your brother get upset when you said you freed his pet?
He said, "My fault, you couldn't guess that all he eats is watercress."	

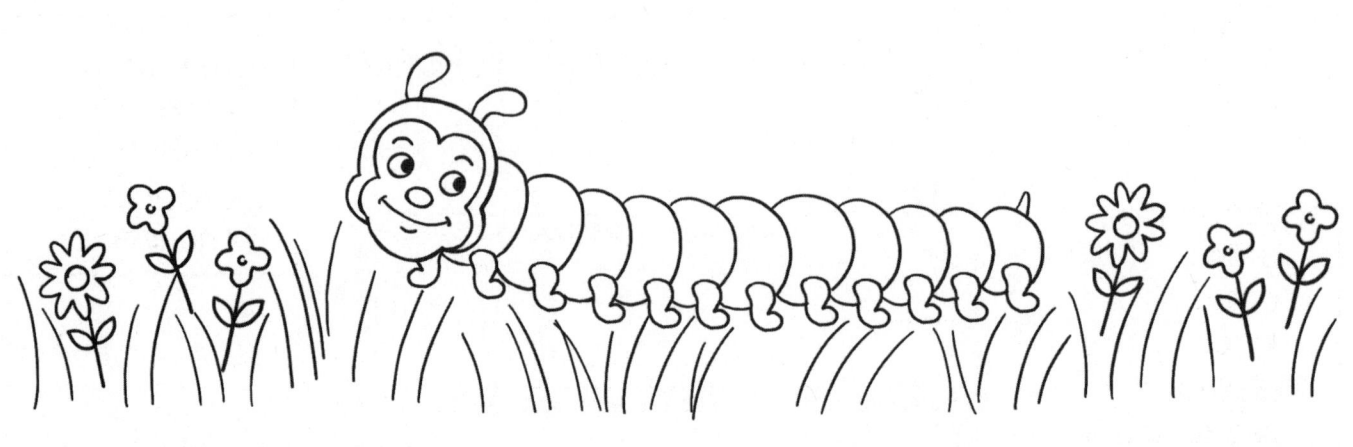

Name _____

WORD LADDER 1
-eed

**Read the clues. Then, write the words.
Start at the bottom and climb to the top.**

Start With a Seed

8. To give food to.
Take away one letter.

7. Let an animal go from a cage; "Yesterday, I ___ the rabbit."
Add one letter.

6. A man's name; short for Frederick.
Add one letter at the beginning.

5. A bright color, like an apple.
Change one letter.

4. Joined in marriage.
Take away one letter.

3. An unwanted plant, like a dandelion.
Change one letter.

2. To want or require something.
Change one letter.

1. Something that is done. "I did a good ___ today."
Change one letter.

s e e d

53

WORD LADDER 2
-eed

Name _____

Read the clues. Then, write the words.
Start at the bottom and climb to the top.

Many-Legged Pet

9. The person who owned the centipede.
Add two letters at the end.

8. A clear soup made from boiling meat or vegetables.
Move the letters around.

7. To beat loudly or quickly, like your heart after running.
Add two letters at the beginning.

6. To steal money from someone.
Change one letter.

5. To cry loudly.
Change one letter.

4. The layer of ground where grass grows.
Take away two vowels. Add one vowel in their place.

3. A plant starts out as this.
Change the last two letters.

2. "Mom ___ me to the store to buy milk."
Change one letter.

1. A penny.
Take away the last five letters.

c e n t i p e d e

MINI-LESSON
-eed

Connect 4 Phonograms

Objective: Partners will play Connect 4 with -eed words.

Materials

- "Never Feed a Centipede" (page 51)
- highlighters
- -eed Connect 4 game board (see right)
- Consonant Letter and Consonant Cluster Cards* (pages 125–127)
- 2 different-colored sheets of paper

*Each pair of children will need the following set of consonants and consonant clusters photocopied on two different color sheets of paper and cut into individual squares: d, f, n, r, s, w, bl, br, cr, fr, gr, sp, st, tw. Each child gets his or her own set of consonant squares plus six blank squares in one color.

(Available online.)

Procedure

1. Invite children to read the poem several times.
2. Ask children to help you highlight the -eed words in the poem. Then, ask them for other -eed words they know.
3. Partner up children, then give each pair a copy of the -eed Connect 4 game board and the letter squares. (Each child chooses one of the two colors.) Have each child place the letter squares in a pile, facedown, on his or her side of the game board.
4. To play, players take turns drawing a letter square. If a player draws a consonant that can be added to -eed to make a word, she can place the consonant on a square on the game board. If a player picks a blank letter card, she may write any letter(s) to make an -eed word and place it on the game board. Both players must agree that the word is correct. The goal is to get four of their color squares in a row.

-eed words		
deed	bleed	**agreed**
feed	breed	indeed
need	creed	ragweed
reed	**freed**	seaweed
seed	greed	**succeed**
weed	speed	
	steed	
	tweed	

Note: You might want to model how to play the game. For instance, pick a consonant square (s) and show how you can lay it on -eed to make a word (seed). Then pick another square (bl) to make another word (bleed) and lay it next to seed to connect two squares, continuing to work toward connecting four squares. (You may want to let children discover for themselves how to play strategically to keep their opponent from connecting four squares.)

Assessment: Circulate as children play to listen as they blend the letter squares with the phonograms on the game board. Did they make words that were correct?

PARTNER POEM -ell

The Shell at the Beach

1st Voice	**2nd Voice**
I went to the beach,	
	Tra-la-tra-la
I went to the beach, and found a shell,	
	And found a shell Tra-la
I went to the beach and found a shell. The shell at the beach did not look well.	
	The shell at the beach did not look well. Tra-la
I went to the beach and found a shell. The shell at the beach did not look well. Dead or alive? Hard to tell.	

(continued)

PARTNER POEM
-ell

1st Voice   **2nd Voice**

Dead or alive?
Hard to tell.
Tra-la-tra-la

I went to the beach
and found a shell.
The shell at the beach
did not look well.
Dead or alive?
Hard to tell.
The shell at the beach
began to smell.

The shell at the beach
began to smell.
Tra-la-tra-la-tra-la

I went to the beach
and found a shell.
The shell at the beach
did not look well.
Dead or alive?
Hard to tell.
The shell at the beach
began to smell.
The story ended
not too well.

The story ended
not too well.
Tra-la-tra-la-tra-la-tra-la
Tra-la-tra-la-tra-la

WORD LADDER 1
-est

Name _____

Read the clues. Then, write the words.
Start at the bottom and climb to the top.

Ride On!

9. The part of the country where cowboys work; opposite of *east*.
Change one letter.

8. A type of jacket without sleeves.
Change one letter.

7. Opposite of *worst*.
Add one letter.

6. To make a guess about what might happen. "If it snows, I ___ we won't have school tomorrow."
Change one letter.

5. A wooden stick used to hit a baseball.
Change one letter.

4. A body of water that is partly closed in by land.
Change one letter.

3. A type of bird; blue___.
Change one letter.

2. A feeling of great happiness.
Change one letter.

1. A young male or lad.
Take away three letters.

c o w b o y

WORD LADDER 2
-est

Name _____

Read the clues. Then, write the words.
Start at the bottom and climb to the top.

Rattle and Roll

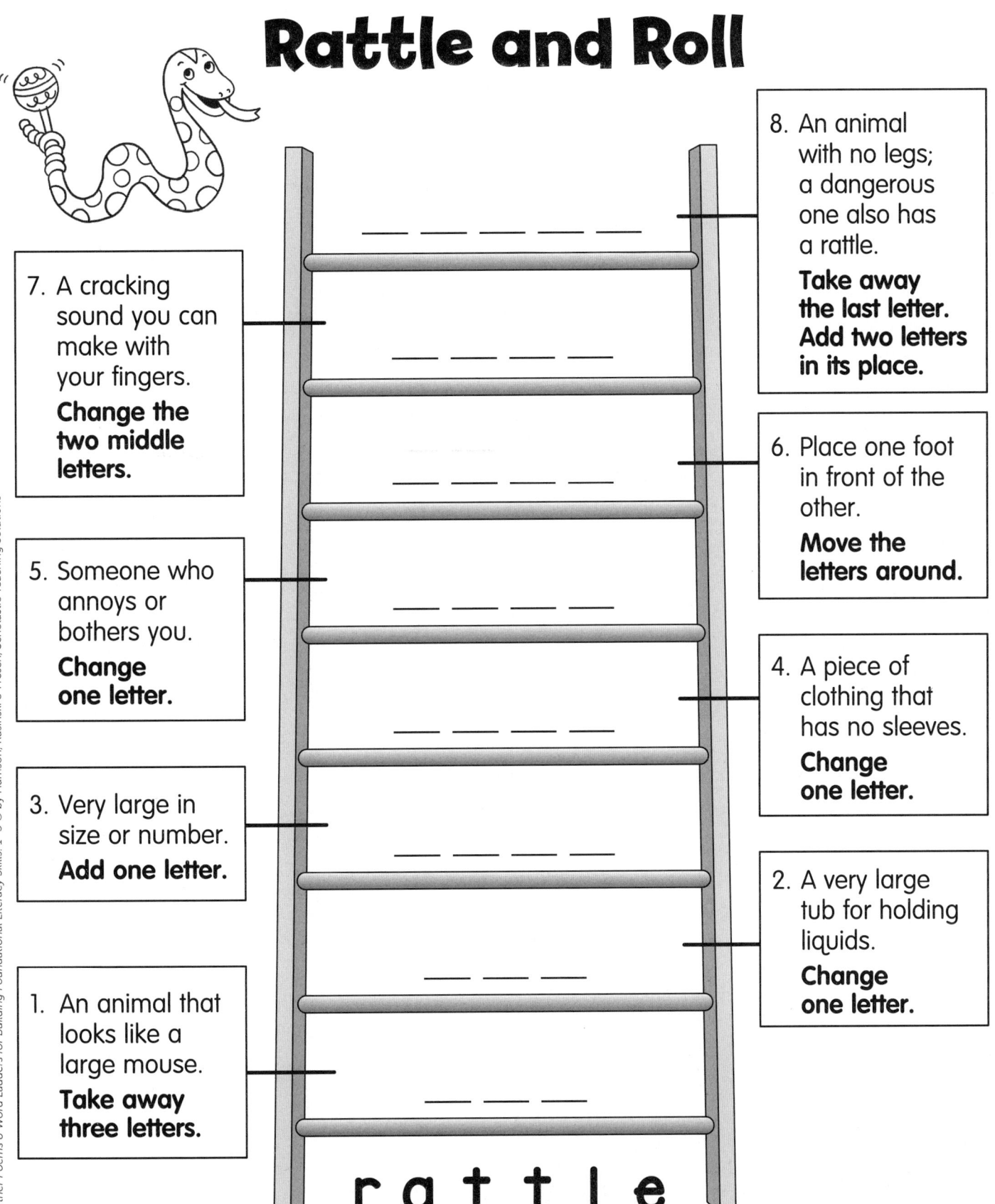

8. An animal with no legs; a dangerous one also has a rattle. **Take away the last letter. Add two letters in its place.**

7. A cracking sound you can make with your fingers. **Change the two middle letters.**

6. Place one foot in front of the other. **Move the letters around.**

5. Someone who annoys or bothers you. **Change one letter.**

4. A piece of clothing that has no sleeves. **Change one letter.**

3. Very large in size or number. **Add one letter.**

2. A very large tub for holding liquids. **Change one letter.**

1. An animal that looks like a large mouse. **Take away three letters.**

r a t t l e

MINI-LESSON
-est

Guessing Game

Objective: Children will write *-est* words based on clues.

Materials
- "I Want to Be a Cowgirl" (page 61)
- highlighters
- paper and pencils

Procedure

1. Invite children to read the poem several times.

2. Have children help you highlight the *-est* words in the poem.

3. Distribute paper and pencils to children. Have children number their paper from 1 to 10.

4. Tell children you will read them a clue about one of the *-est* words from the poem. They will guess what each word is. To help them understand the clues, you might want to ask them to help you define a few words; for example, "What does *best* mean?"

5. Read aloud each clue below and have children write the word on their paper. They may use the poem as a reference for correct spelling. (Note that the last three clues are your own. You can pick words from the chart below.)

Clues:

1. This is a place where birds live. (*nest*)
2. A direction that is opposite of east. (*west*)
3. When I take a nap I ____. (*rest*)
4. If you come stay at my house but do not live there, you are my ____. (*guest*)
5. Not the worst but the ____. (*best*)
6. A jacket without sleeves. (*vest*)
7. Someone or something that is a bother. (*pest*)
8–10. Your choice

-est words		
best	blest	arrest
fest	chest	contest
jest	crest	detest
lest	**guest**	digest
nest	quest	forest
pest		honest
rest		ingest
test		modest
vest		
west		
zest		

Assessment: Do children understand the clues and write the correct *-est* words? Are they able to correctly write the three *-est* words that were not in the poem?

Just for "Ew"

1st Voice | **2nd Voice**

Of all the words that end in "ew,"
I could only find a few
to write this poem just for you.

"You" sounds the same as "ew,"
so it's okay to use a "you."

Okay, a "you" can be an "ew,"
but can I also use a "true?"

You can use a true for "ew,"
like flew and grew, chew and crew,
knew and blew, to name a few.

That's so good to know. Whew!
I was in a real stew.
I couldn't tell what I should do.
I thought each word must end in "ew."

Glad to help.

Glad you knew.

Love my poem.

Thanks to you!

WORD LADDER 1
-ew

Name _____

Read the clues. Then, write the words. Start at the bottom and climb to the top.

It's True!

8. "My plant ___ tall this summer."
Change one letter.

7. A group of people who work together.
Change one letter.

6. "Yesterday I ___ a picture of my family."
Add one letter.

5. Small drops of water on grass in the morning.
Change one letter.

4. Not many.
Take away one letter.

3. Past tense of *fly*. "Yesterday, I ___ in a plane."
Change one letter.

2. "Yesterday the wind ___ down a tree."
Change last two letters.

1. The color of the sky.
Change the first two letters.

t r u e

Name _____

WORD LADDER 2
-ew

**Read the clues. Then, write the words.
Start at the bottom and climb to the top.**

Let's Eat!

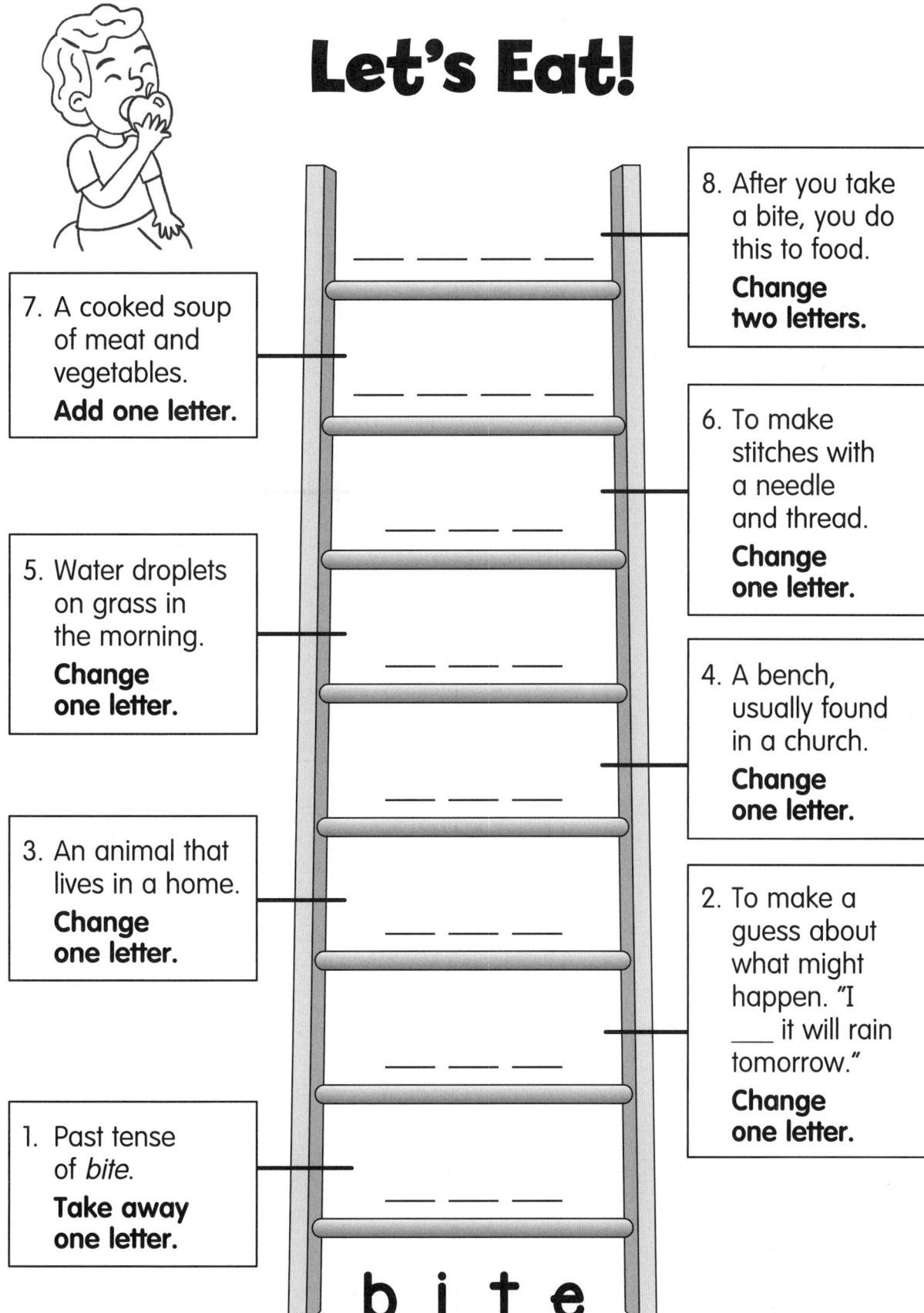

8. After you take a bite, you do this to food.
Change two letters.

7. A cooked soup of meat and vegetables.
Add one letter.

6. To make stitches with a needle and thread.
Change one letter.

5. Water droplets on grass in the morning.
Change one letter.

4. A bench, usually found in a church.
Change one letter.

3. An animal that lives in a home.
Change one letter.

2. To make a guess about what might happen. "I ___ it will rain tomorrow."
Change one letter.

1. Past tense of *bite*.
Take away one letter.

b i t e

67

Acrostic Sentences

MINI-LESSON
-ew

Objective: Children will write acrostic sentences with *-ew* words.

Materials
- "Just for 'Ew'" (page 65)
- highlighters
- whiteboard or chart paper
- paper and pencils

Procedure

1. Read the poem several times with children.

2. Have children help highlight the *-ew* words in the poem.

3. Write the word BLEW vertically on the left-hand side of a whiteboard or chart paper. Invite children to help you create a word bank by brainstorming several words for each letter in the word (for example: b = *banana, bread, Barry*; l = *letter, learn, left*; e = *exit, egg, early*; w = *worm, walk, Wednesday*). Write the words at the bottom of the page.

4. Next, have children help you create an acrostic sentence using the brainstormed words. For example:
    Barry
    Left
    Early
    Wednesday

5. Distribute paper and pencils to children. Ask them to choose one of the highlighted *-ew* words in the poem. Have them write the letters vertically down the left-hand side of the paper.

6. Ask children to create a word bank at the bottom of their page by brainstorming words for each letter. (You can set a number of words, such as "at least three" or "more than four.")

7. Have children create an acrostic sentence using their word bank. Then, invite them to share their sentences.

Assessment: Check children's word banks for vocabulary and spelling. Did they think of enough words? How conventional are their spellings?

-ew words		
dew	**blew**	askew
few	brew	brand-new
hew	**chew**	corkscrew
Jew	**crew**	honeydew
mew	drew	interview
new	**flew**	nephew
pew	**grew**	overview
yew	**knew**	preview
	screw	withdrew
	shrew	
	slew	
	stew	
	strew	
	threw	
	whew	

Beware of Mice

1st Voice	2nd Voice
I don't think that mice are nice.	
	Allow me to explain.
If you have mice, take my advice.	
	Better hide your grain.
To be precise, they'll eat your rice.	
	No nibble will remain.
Think it over once or twice.	
	Mice are just a pain.
Having mice, you pay a price.	
	They'll drive you quite insane.
I don't think that mice are nice.	
	They'll drive you quite insane.

WORD LADDER 1
-ice

Name _____

Read the clues. Then, write the words.
Start at the bottom and climb to the top.

What Mice Are Not

9. Opposite of *mean*; mice are not this.
Change one letter.

8. Small cubes with dots on each side; used in games.
Change one letter.

7. To eat at dinnertime.
Change one letter.

6. A type of evergreen tree with cones.
Change one letter.

5. A long, thin mark made by a pen or pencil.
Change one letter.

4. A street or avenue.
Change one letter.

3. A thin clothing material with holes and fancy stitches.
Change one letter.

2. A contest of speed, such as running.
Change one letter.

1. A type of food grain.
Change one letter.

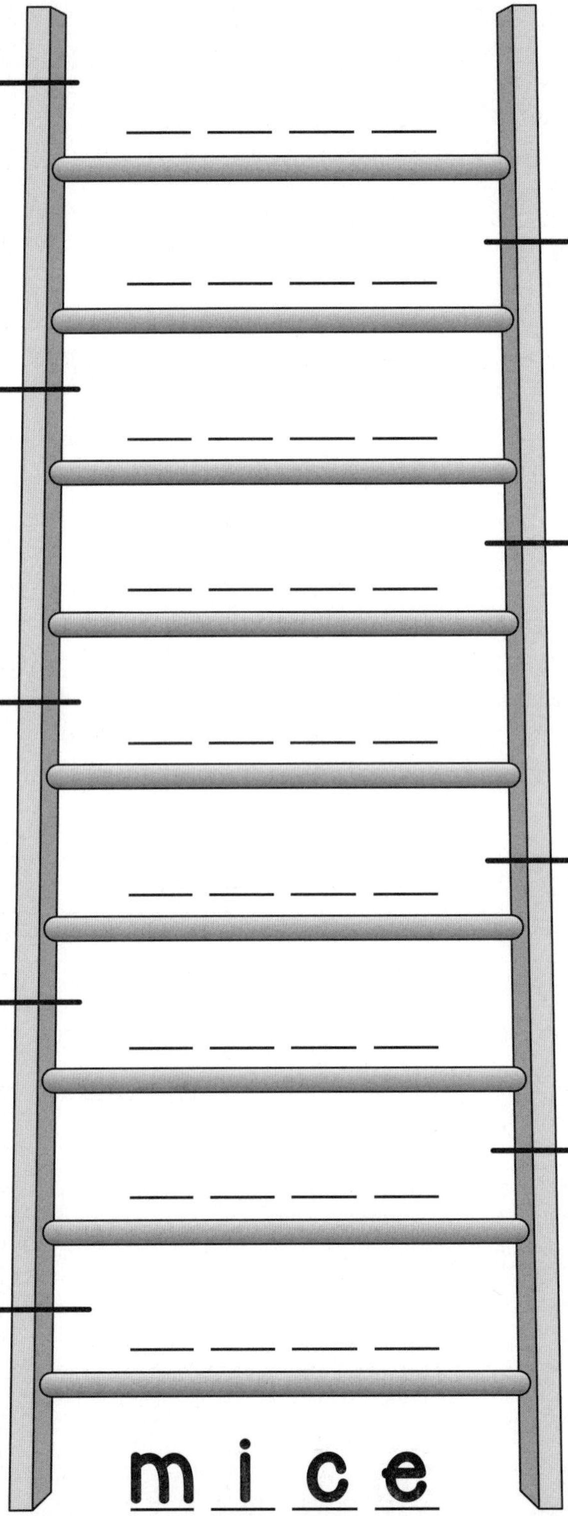

m i c e

Name _____

Read the clues. Then, write the words. Start at the bottom and climb to the top.

WORD LADDER 2
-ice

Mad Mice

9. Crazy; mice can drive you ___.
   Add two letters at the beginning.

8. To have good sense and judgement.
   Change one letter.

7. A wise person.
   Add one letter at the beginning.

6. A period of life measured in years.
   Take away one letter.

5. A sheet of paper in a book or magazine.
   Change one letter.

4. Great anger.
   Change one letter.

3. A speed contest, like with cars or running.
   Take away two letters. Add one letter in their place.

2. Where astronauts travel.
   Change one letter.

1. Seasonings used to add flavor to food.
   Take away one letter. Add two letters in its place.

m i c e

71

MINI-LESSON -ice

Going on a Word Hunt

Objective: Children will play a game using the *-ice* and *-ain* words.

Materials
- "Beware of Mice" (page 69)
- highlighters
- Word Hunt cards (see right)

Procedure

1. Invite children to read the poem several times.
2. Have children help highlight the *-ice* and *-ain* words in the poem.
3. Tell children that they will be going on a Word Hunt. To find each word, they'll need to know what it means.
4. Ask children to define the following words: *mice, price, nice, rice, twice, advice, pain, remain, explain.*
5. Pair up children and give each pair a Word Hunt card. Explain that partners will have to listen to figure out if they have the next card in the hunt.
6. Invite the pair with the first card to read it aloud. Then, ask the group which poem word means "small rodents." The pair with the card that matches that answer ("I have MICE . . .") reads their card next, and so on.
7. Continue the game until the last card is read, providing support as needed.

Assessment: Listen as partners discuss if their card is next in the hunt. Note which children need assistance with the definitions.

Going on a Word Hunt

I have the **first card**. I'm going on a Word Hunt for the word that means "small rodents."	I have **TWICE**. I'm going on a Word Hunt for the word that means "suggestion of what to do."
I have **MICE**. I'm going on a Word Hunt for the word that means "cost."	I have **ADVICE**. I'm going on a Word Hunt for the word that means "a feeling that hurts."
I have **PRICE**. I'm going on a Word Hunt for the word that means "something pleasant."	I have **PAIN**. I'm going on a Word Hunt for the word that means "stay."
I have **NICE**. I'm going on a Word Hunt for the word that means "a food that is a side dish."	I have **REMAIN**. I'm going on a Word Hunt for the word that means "to make an idea clear."
I have **RICE**. I'm going on a Word Hunt for the word that means "two times."	I have **EXPLAIN**, and I have the last card!

(Available online.)

-ice words

dice	**price**	**advice**
lice	slice	device
mice	spice	entice
nice	splice	precise
rice	thrice	
vice	**twice**	

PARTNER POEM
-ick

The Tick That Liked Cookies

1st Voice　　　　**2nd Voice**

There once was
　an odd little tick,

who said biting dogs
　made him sick.

　　　　　　　　He spent all his money
　　　　　　　　　on biscuits and honey

and cones of ice cream
　he could lick.

　　　　　　　　If you asked him,
　　　　　　　　　his answer was quick.

　　　　　　　　"I'd rather eat brick
　　　　　　　　　or a stick."

And then he'd repeat,
　"A cookie's a treat."

　　　　　　　　Which made him
　　　　　　　　　an odd little tick.

Name _____

WORD LADDER 1
-ick

**Read the clues. Then, write the words.
Start at the bottom and climb to the top.**

Don't Bug Me!

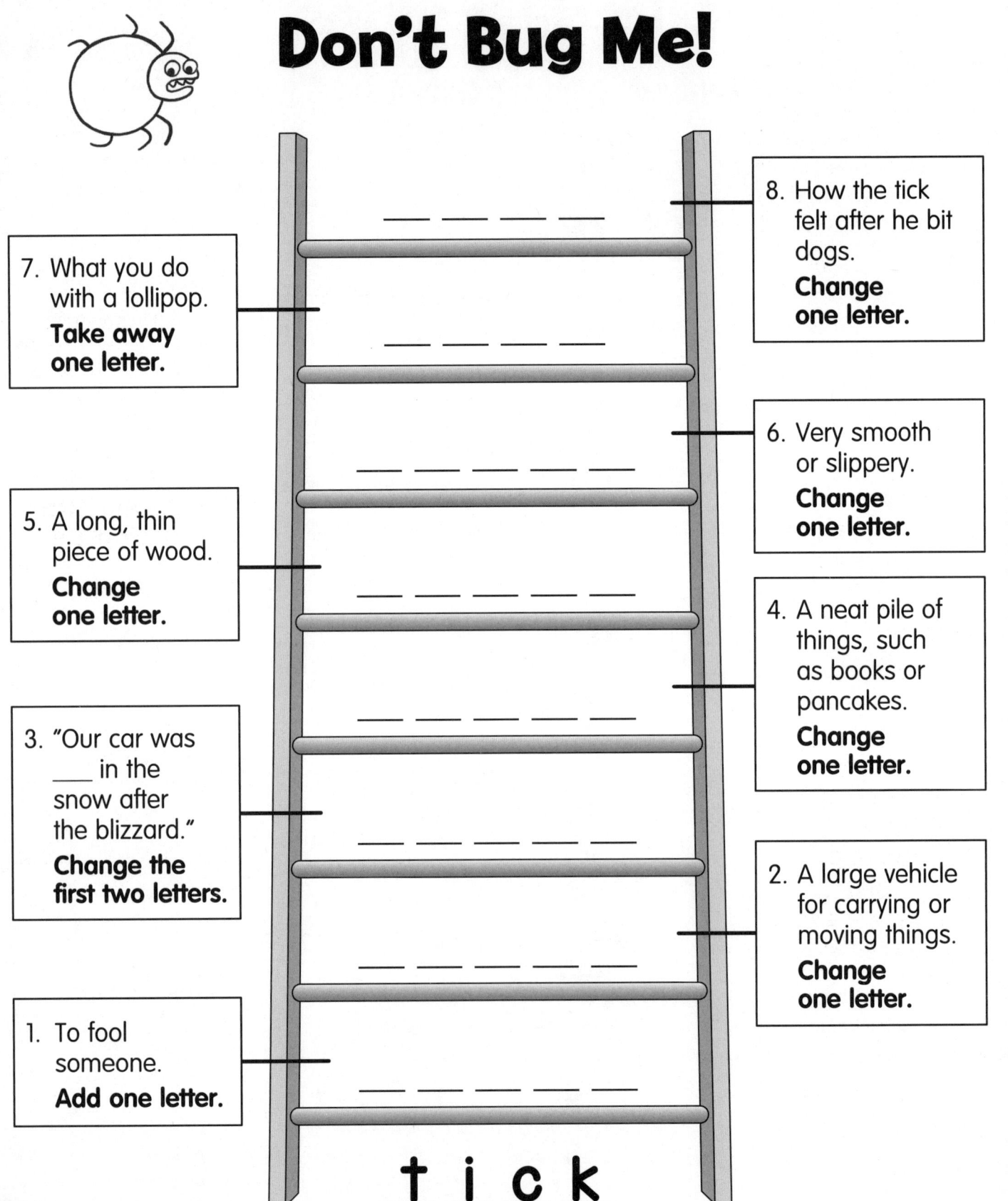

8. How the tick felt after he bit dogs. **Change one letter.**

7. What you do with a lollipop. **Take away one letter.**

6. Very smooth or slippery. **Change one letter.**

5. A long, thin piece of wood. **Change one letter.**

4. A neat pile of things, such as books or pancakes. **Change one letter.**

3. "Our car was ___ in the snow after the blizzard." **Change the first two letters.**

2. A large vehicle for carrying or moving things. **Change one letter.**

1. To fool someone. **Add one letter.**

t i c k

Name _____

WORD LADDER 2
-ick

**Read the clues. Then, write the words.
Start at the bottom and climb to the top.**

Cool Treat!

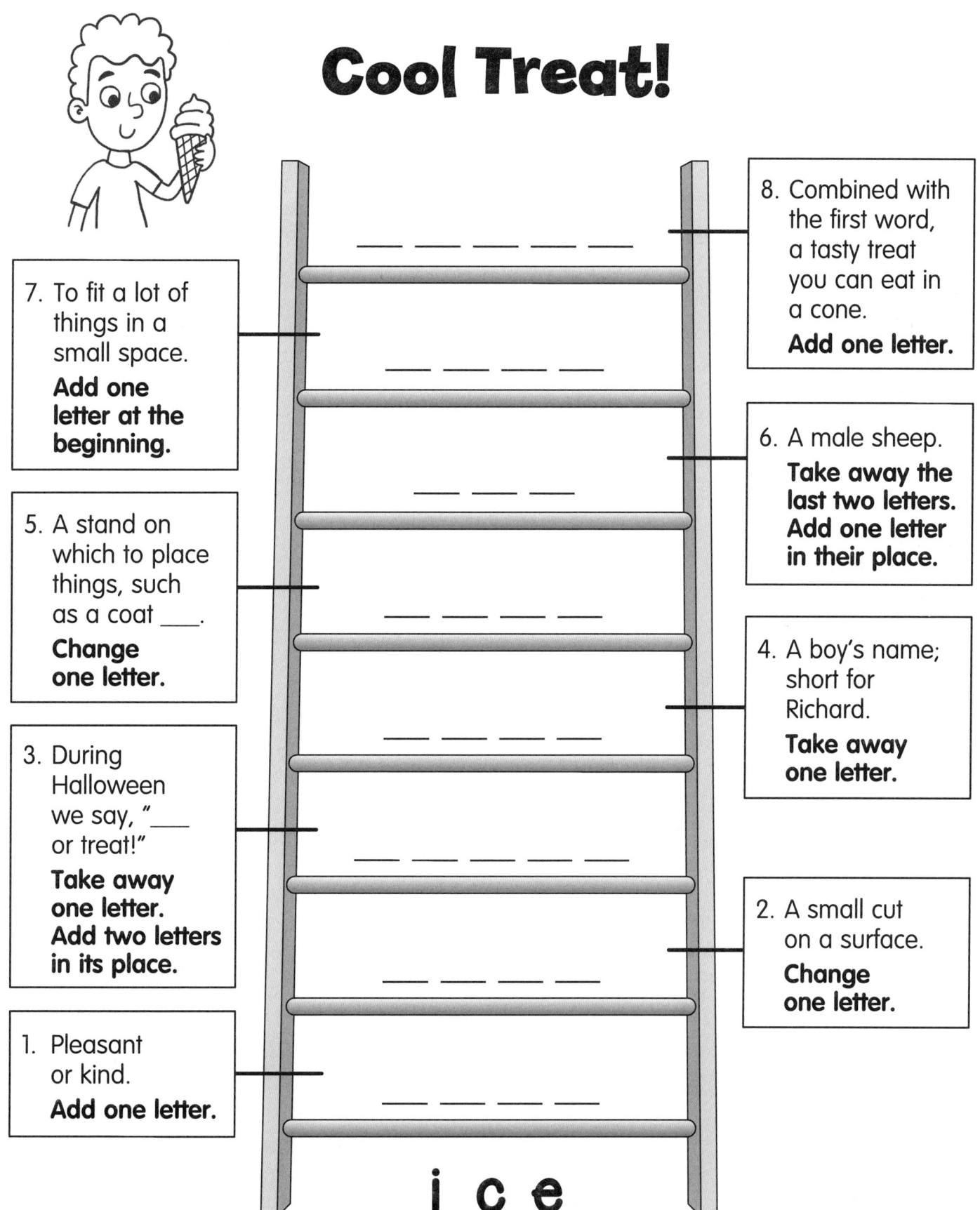

8. Combined with the first word, a tasty treat you can eat in a cone. **Add one letter.**

7. To fit a lot of things in a small space. **Add one letter at the beginning.**

6. A male sheep. **Take away the last two letters. Add one letter in their place.**

5. A stand on which to place things, such as a coat ___. **Change one letter.**

4. A boy's name; short for Richard. **Take away one letter.**

3. During Halloween we say, "___ or treat!" **Take away one letter. Add two letters in its place.**

2. A small cut on a surface. **Change one letter.**

1. Pleasant or kind. **Add one letter.**

i c e

75

MINI-LESSON
-ick

Fish Stick

Objective: Children will play a game to make *-ick* words using craft sticks and a fish card.

Materials
- "The Tick That Liked Cookies" (page 73)
- highlighters
- chart paper
- craft sticks (one per child)
- markers
- paper and pencils
- Fish Stick cards (see right)

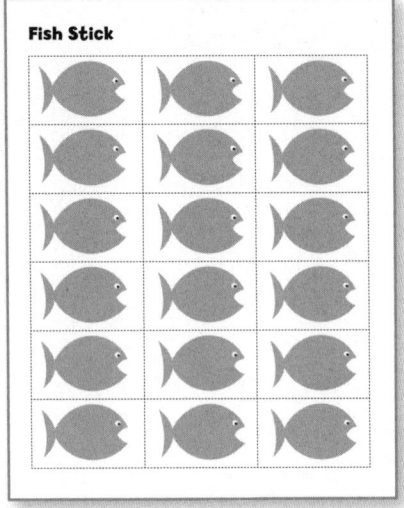

(Available online.)

Procedure

1. Read the poem with children several times.
2. Have children highlight the *-ick* words in the poem.
3. Ask them to help brainstorm more words with the *-ick* phonogram. (See table at right for ideas.) List their words on chart paper.
4. Give each child a craft stick. Ask children to write *-ick* on their stick.
5. Divide the class into small groups of four or five children. Give each group a sheet of paper and tell them to list 18 *-ick* words. They can use the highlighted and brainstormed words for reference.
6. Give each group a set of 18 Fish Stick cards. Ask children to write the beginning consonant or blend/digraph of the first word on a fish. (For example, for the word *brick*, they would write *br* on the fish.) Have them repeat for all 18 words. When they have finished, have children place the cards facedown.
7. Children in each group take turns picking a card and laying their stick next to it. In order to "catch" the fish, a child must correctly tell the group the word he created. Otherwise, the child returns the card in the facedown fish pile to be "caught" again later. Play continues until all fish are caught.

-ick words		
kick	**brick**	homesick
lick	chick	lipstick
Mick	click	toothpick
Nick	crick	
pick	flick	
Rick	**quick**	
sick	slick	
tick	snick	
wick	**stick**	
	thick	
	trick	

Assessment: Listen as children play the game. Who can successfully blend the onsets (consonants/blends or digraphs) and the *-ick* rime?

Poor Clyde

PARTNER POEM -ide

1st Voice	All Together	2nd Voice
I can't find Clyde.		
		He can't find Clyde.
	Here, Clyde.	
I've tried and tried		
		To find Clyde.
	Here, Clyde.	
	Here, Clyde.	
I've looked inside.		
		He's looked outside.
	Where, oh, where would Clyde hide?	
I've looked far.		
		He's looked wide.
	Could Clyde have died?	
"Oh, no!" I cried.		
		He cried and cried.
	Poor Clyde has died!	
I miss my fish!		
		A fish?
	Clyde's a fish!	
I see his bowl.		
		He sees his fish!
Oh, yay!		
		Oh, joy!
	Clyde is found. He got his wish!	

WORD LADDER 1
-ide

Name _____

**Read the clues. Then, write the words.
Start at the bottom and climb to the top.**

Where We Searched

8. Opposite of *near*; the poet searched for Clyde "___ and wide." **Take away one letter.**

7. The cost of riding on a bus, train, or plane. **Change one letter.**

6. The light, heat, and flames produced by burning. **Change one letter.**

5. The rubber around the wheel of a car. **Change one letter.**

4. The rising and falling of the sea level. **Change one letter.**

3. What you do in a car. **Take away one letter.**

2. To be proud of oneself; also, a family of lions. **Take away one letter. Add two letters in its place.**

1. To go where you can't be seen. **Change one letter.**

w i d e

Name _____

WORD LADDER 2
-ide

Read the clues. Then, write the words.
Start at the bottom and climb to the top.

My Pet Clyde

9. An animal that lives in water; Clyde is a ___.
   Change one letter.

7. Having good sense or judgment.
   Change one letter.

5. The right or left part of the body. "I sleep on my right ___."
   Change one letter.

3. To lose energy; also, the rubber cover of a wheel.
   Change the "u" to "i." Then move the letters around.

1. Something that helps solve a mystery.
   Take away "yd." Add one letter in its place.

8. To want or hope for something to happen.
   Change one letter.

6. A measurement across from one side to another. "My desk is 3 feet ___."
   Change one letter.

4. The change in sea level, caused by the pull of the sun and the moon.
   Change one letter.

2. Opposite of *false*.
   Change the first two letters.

C l y d e

MINI-LESSON
-ide

Hide the Words

Objective: Children will write *-ide* words to exchange with buddies.

Materials
- "Poor Clyde" (page 77)
- highlighters
- chart paper
- white paper
- white crayon
- watercolor paint
- paintbrush

Procedure

1. Invite children to read the poem several times.
2. Have children highlight the *-ide* words in the poem.
3. Ask them to help brainstorm more words with the *-ide* phonogram. (See table at right for ideas.) List their words on chart paper, where children can view them.
4. Distribute paper and white crayons to children. Ask children to choose 10 words from the list and write each one on their paper, using the crayon.
5. Pair up children and have partners exchange papers. Invite children to use watercolor paint to paint over the paper to reveal the words. Ask: *Did you and your partner choose any of the same words?*
6. Invite children to read aloud the words they revealed.

-ide words		
bide	bride	abide
hide	chide	aside
ride	glide	beside
side	guide	Clyde
tide	oxide	collide
wide	pride	confide
	slide	decide
	snide	divide
	stride	**inside**
		outside
		provide
		reside
		rawhide
		upside

Assessment: Are children able to correctly spell the *-ide* words they chose? Listen for correctness as children read aloud the words. Do they need assistance or further support with any words?

Wondering About *Clyde*?

We often find that names do not follow phonic rules. The origins of names often have a relationship to a particular culture or part of the world. *Clyde* is Scottish in origin. The River Clyde is the most famous river in Scotland. The area is also famous for Clydesdale horses.

PARTNER POEM
-ight

My Wish Tonight

| **1st Voice** | **2nd Voice** | **3rd Voice** |

Wishing on this silent night,
grass soft beneath my head,

    Star light
    Star bright

        Can you find my grassy bed
        looking down from such a height?

    First star
    I see tonight

Wishing star with light so bright,
will you grant a wish for me,

    I wish I may
    I wish I might

        Just one tiny wish for free
        before the sky fills up with light?

    Have the wish
    I wish tonight

I hope that what they say is right,
when I wish and close my eyes,

        You'll look down from starry skies
        and I will have my wish tonight.

WORD LADDER 1
-ight

Name _____

**Read the clues. Then, write the words.
Start at the bottom and climb to the top.**

A Light in the Dark

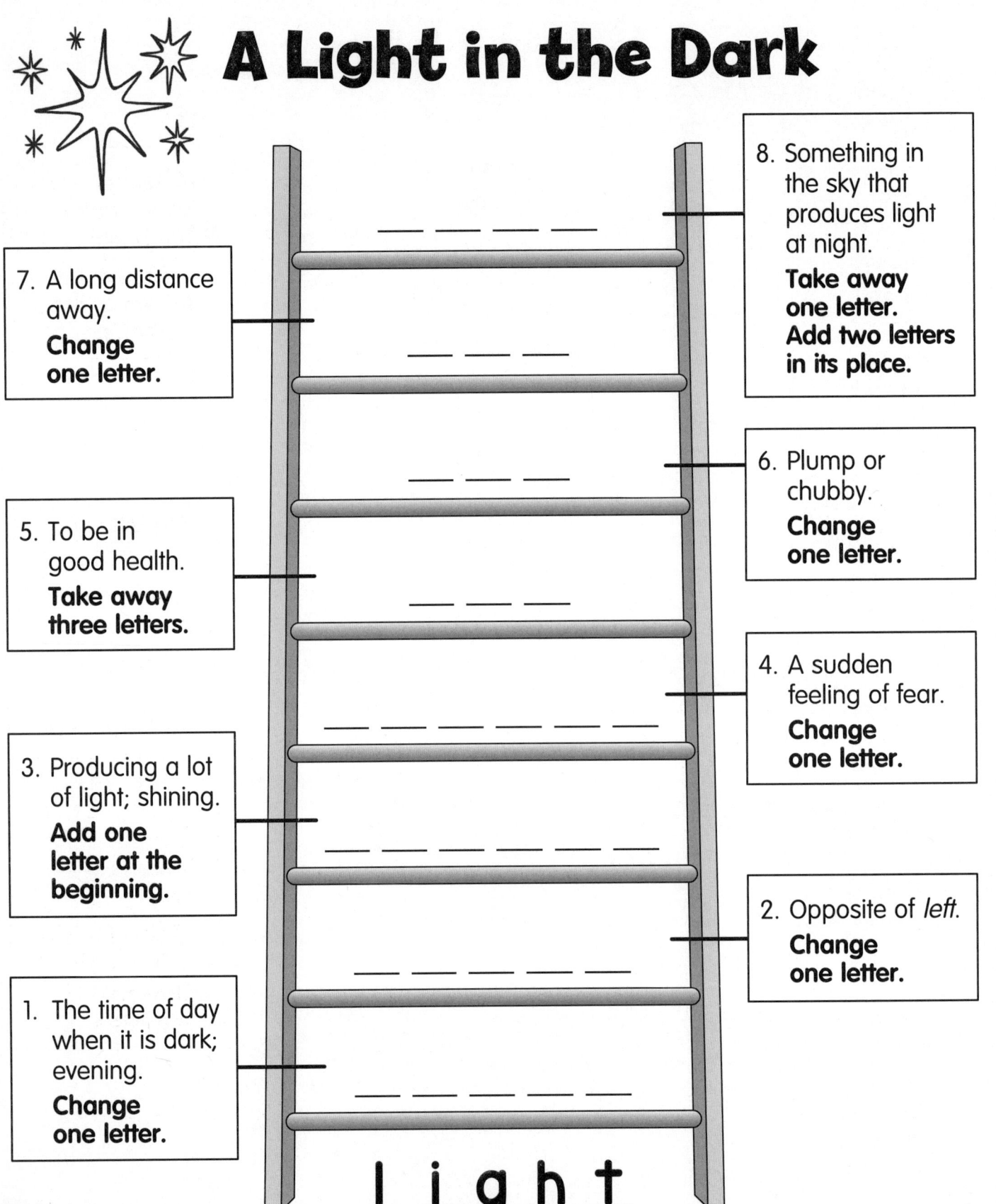

8. Something in the sky that produces light at night.
Take away one letter. Add two letters in its place.

7. A long distance away.
Change one letter.

6. Plump or chubby.
Change one letter.

5. To be in good health.
Take away three letters.

4. A sudden feeling of fear.
Change one letter.

3. Producing a lot of light; shining.
Add one letter at the beginning.

2. Opposite of *left*.
Change one letter.

1. The time of day when it is dark; evening.
Change one letter.

l i g h t

WORD LADDER 2
-ight

Name _____

Read the clues. Then, write the words.
Start at the bottom and climb to the top.

I Wish I May . . .

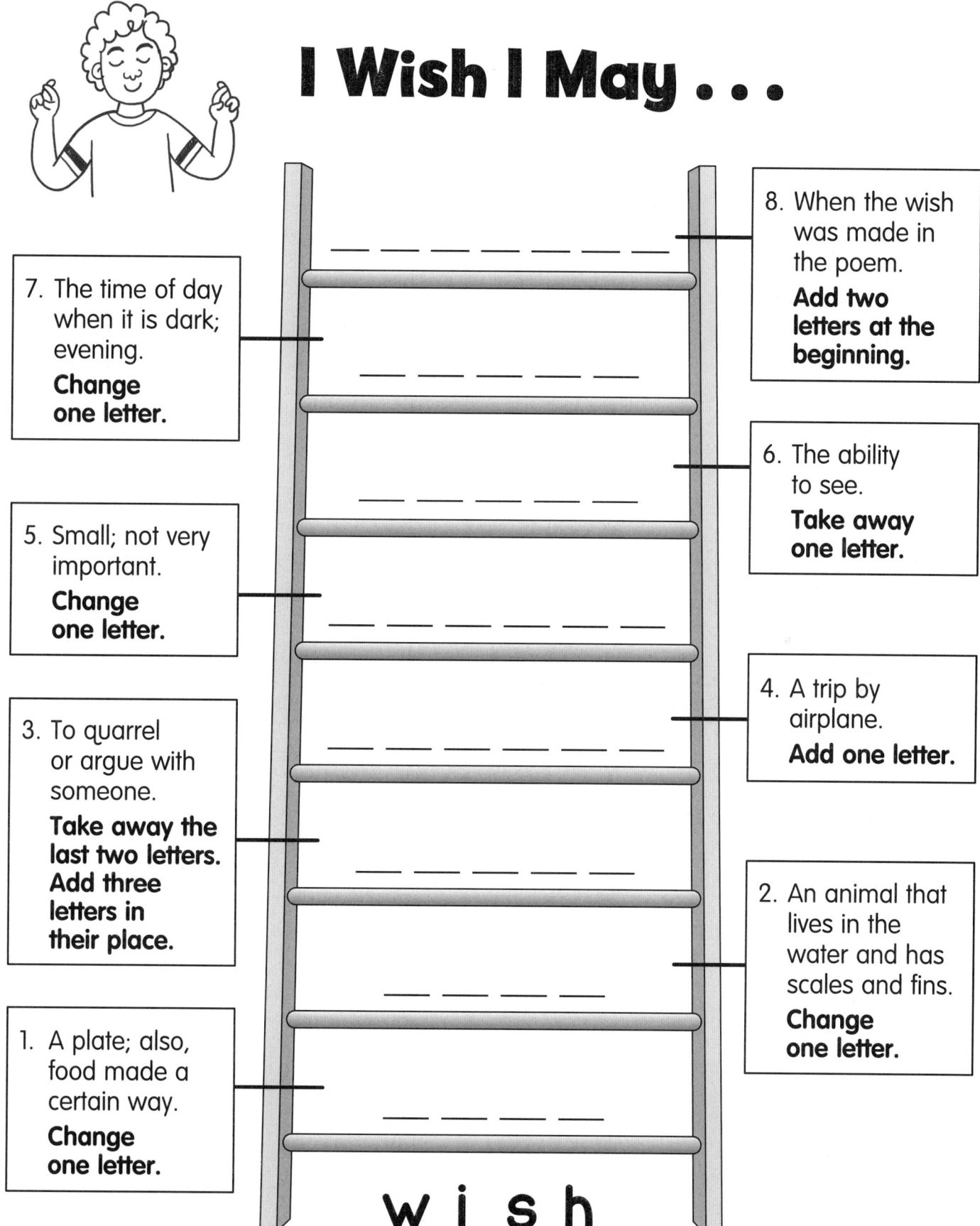

8. When the wish was made in the poem.
Add two letters at the beginning.

7. The time of day when it is dark; evening.
Change one letter.

6. The ability to see.
Take away one letter.

5. Small; not very important.
Change one letter.

4. A trip by airplane.
Add one letter.

3. To quarrel or argue with someone.
Take away the last two letters. Add three letters in their place.

2. An animal that lives in the water and has scales and fins.
Change one letter.

1. A plate; also, food made a certain way.
Change one letter.

w i s h

MINI-LESSON
-ight

Word Construction

Objective: Children will help connect letters to the *-ight* phonogram to make words.

Materials
- "My Wish Tonight" (page 81)
- highlighters
- chart paper
- Word Construction cards (see right)

Procedure
1. Read the poem several times with children.
2. Have children help highlight the *-ight* words.
3. Ask children to help brainstorm more words with the *-ight* phonogram. (See table at right for ideas.) List their words on chart paper, where children can view them.
4. Divide the class into small groups of three or four children. Pass out a set of Word Construction cards to each group.
5. Have children spread out the cards on their table so they can see all the letters. Ask each group to take the *r* card and place it next to an *ight* card. Ask children: *What word does it make?* (right) Have children look at all the other cards. Ask: *What other letter or word can you add to the beginning of* right *to make another word?* (Possible answers: *f, b, up*)
6. Have children continue to use the letter cards to make five more *-ight* words. You can do this as a directed whole-class activity or have children work in their groups, then bring together to share their words. (Possible words: *right/fright/bright; light/flight/blight/plight/starlight/delight; night/knight/tonight/midnight; tight/uptight; sight/slight*)

Word Construction

m	b	r	l	f
s	p	k	n	t
de	mid	star	up	to
ight	ight	ight	ight	ight

(Available online.)

-ight words		
fight	blight	delight
light	**bright**	downright
might	flight	**height**
night	fright	midnight
right	knight	starlight
sight	plight	**tonight**
tight	slight	uptight

Assessment: Observe which children contribute to the activity. Who are able to combine letters to create *-ight* words?

Wondering about *height*?

Do you pronounce this word as if there is a *th* at the end? That pronunciation is common, thanks to a competing spelling of the word into the 18th century (*heighth, highth*). The proper pronunciation today rhymes with *right*. Read more at https://www.merriam-webster.com/words-at-play/the-height-of-mispronunciation2014or-not.

PARTNER POEM
-ine

Careful, Little Fish

1st Voice	**2nd Voice**	**3rd Voice**
Little fish, feeling fine,		
		Bright water, sunshine,
Worm wiggles on a vine.		
	Careful, little fish.	
Don't be fooled by fake vine.		
		Worm makes you want to dine.
Don't get caught on fishing line.		
	Careful, little fish.	
Bright metal, warning sign,		
		Hidden hook, number nine,
Will jerk you up in the sunshine.		
	Careful, little fish.	
		Don't let someone else feel fine.
Don't let someone get to dine.		
		Leave the worm still on the line.
	Bye-bye, little fish.	

WORD LADDER 1
-ine

Name _____

**Read the clues. Then, write the words.
Start at the bottom and climb to the top.**

Take Care

8. The character in the poem who was told to be careful.
Change two letters.

7. Very good. "I feel ___."
Take away two letters. Add one letter in their place.

6. A person or animal's backbone.
Add one letter.

5. A type of evergreen tree with cones.
Change one letter.

4. A sheet of glass in a window; sounds like *pain*.
Change one letter.

3. A narrow street.
Change one letter.

2. A stick used to help with walking.
Change one letter.

1. To feel interest or be concerned about someone or something.
Take away three letters.

c a r e f u l

WORD LADDER 2
-ine

Name _____

Read the clues. Then, write the words.
Start at the bottom and climb to the top.

What's for Dinner?

8. The animal that the fish wanted to dine on. **Change one letter.**

7. Old clothes that have been used for a long time look ___. **Add one letter.**

6. "Last night, our team ___ the baseball game." **Change one letter.**

5. To finish first in a race. **Take away one letter.**

4. A drink made from grapes, for grown-ups. **Take away one letter.**

3. To complain in a high-pitched voice. **Change one letter.**

2. To give off a bright light, like the sun. **Take away one letter. Add two letters in its place.**

1. Something that belongs to me. **Change one letter.**

d i n e

MINI-LESSON
-ine

Four in a Line

Objective: Children will read and match *-ine* words.

Materials

- "Careful, Little Fish" (page 85)
- highlighters
- 2 copies of Four in a Line grid* (for each pair of children; see right)
- two different colors of markers (for each pair of children)

* Cut apart one of the word grids to create a set of word cards for children.

Four in a Line

dine	pine	shine	whine
fine	vine	shrine	airline
line	wine	spine	online
nine	twine	swine	feline

(Available online.)

Procedure

1. Invite children to read the poem several times.
2. Have children help highlight the *-ine* words in the poem.
3. Pair up children and give each pair a Four in a Line grid and a set of the word cards. Shuffle the cards and place them facedown between partners. Give each child in a pair a different color marker.
4. Partners take turns drawing a card and reading the word on it. If the partner agrees that the reader has read the word correctly, the reader uses her marker to make an X on the matching word on the grid. If the reader does not read the word correctly, she returns the card to the bottom of the pile.

-ine words		
dine	shine	airline
fine	shrine	alkaline
line	spine	bovine
nine	swine	equine
pine	twine	feline
vine	whine	iodine
wine		online
		refine
		sunshine

5. The first child to mark four words in a line (across, down, or diagonally) wins. If partners have used up all the cards and neither child has four in a row, have children count their Xs to see who has marked more words. If both children have the same number of words, declare a tie.

Note: You can simplify the game by creating your own grid using only the words in the first two columns in the table above. Repeat some of the words on the grid to fill the 16 boxes. You can also make the game more challenging by using only the words in the third column.

Assessment: Listen in as partners play the game. Who can identify the words and who might need more support or practice with the words?

How Not to Build a Boat

PARTNER POEM *-oat*

1st Voice	All Together	2nd Voice

1st Voice:
From my friend
I got a note,
and this is what
my friend wrote.

2nd Voice:
"What a boring,
rainy day.
Let's build a boat.
What do you say?"

1st Voice:
I wrote my friend,
"What kind of boat?"
My friend wrote back,

2nd Voice:
"A riverboat."

1st Voice:
"A riverboat's
too big," I wrote.
"Let's think about
a smaller boat."
He wrote,

(continued)

PARTNER POEM
-oat

1st Voice	All Together	2nd Voice

2nd Voice:
*"Okay,
a nice rowboat—
small but big
enough to float."*

1st Voice:
Dressed in boots
and new raincoat,
I joined my friend
to build a boat.

and fancy wood,
we built the sides,

2nd Voice:
With lots of paint

And they looked good!

1st Voice: Forgot one thing,

2nd Voice: *So our rowboat stank.*

All Together:
**Without a bottom—
glub glub—
our rowboat sank.**

WORD LADDER 1
-oat

Name _____

Read the clues. Then, write the words. Start at the bottom and climb to the top.

Boat Ride

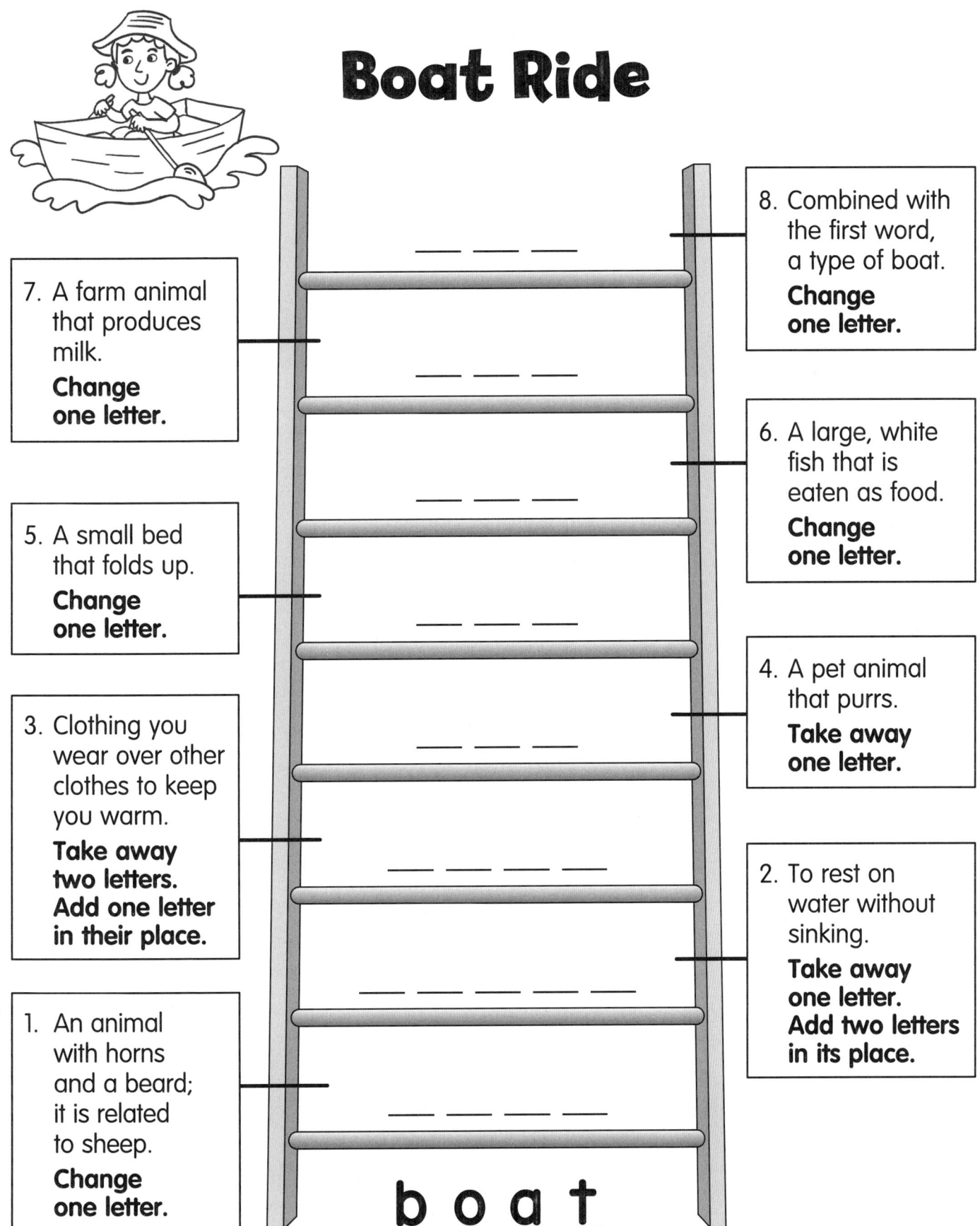

8. Combined with the first word, a type of boat. **Change one letter.**

7. A farm animal that produces milk. **Change one letter.**

6. A large, white fish that is eaten as food. **Change one letter.**

5. A small bed that folds up. **Change one letter.**

4. A pet animal that purrs. **Take away one letter.**

3. Clothing you wear over other clothes to keep you warm. **Take away two letters. Add one letter in their place.**

2. To rest on water without sinking. **Take away one letter. Add two letters in its place.**

1. An animal with horns and a beard; it is related to sheep. **Change one letter.**

b o a t

WORD LADDER 2
-oat

Name _____

Read the clues. Then, write the words.
Start at the bottom and climb to the top.

Warm and Dry

9. Combined with the first word, a type of coat. **Change one letter.**

8. A physical hurt. **Take away one letter.**

7. A liquid used to color walls. **Change one letter.**

6. The sharp end of something. **Take away the "u." Add two letters in its place.**

5. To push out the lips to show that you are not happy. **Add one letter at the beginning.**

4. Opposite of *in*. **Change one letter.**

3. A kind of grain that people and animals eat. **Take away three letters.**

2. The front of the neck. **Take away the first two letters. Add three letters in their place.**

1. To be happy about your own good luck or someone else's bad luck. **Take away one letter. Add two letters in its place.**

c o a t

92

MINI-LESSON
-oat

Word Organizer

Objective: Children will complete graphic organizers for the *-oat* words.

Materials
- "How <u>Not</u> to Build a Boat" (page 89)
- highlighters
- chart paper
- pens or pencils
- Word Work graphic organizer (see right)

Procedure
1. Read the poem several times with children.
2. Have children highlight all the *-oat* words in the poem.
3. Ask them to help brainstorm more words with the *-oat* phonogram. (See table for ideas.) List their words on chart paper, where children can view them.
4. Pair up children and give each pair a copy of the Word Work graphic organizer. Invite children to choose any *-oat* word from the list and complete their graphic organizer.
5. If partners finish quickly, ask them to take a second graphic organizer and complete it with another word.
6. Have children share and post their organizers.

Note: You can use the graphic organizer from this lesson to review any of the phonogram words that children have already examined. Leave copies of the organizer at a workstation along with some of the other word charts you have created so children can complete this organizer independently.

Assessment: Listen in as partners complete their graphic organizers. Which pairs move on to complete a second organizer? Which children might need more support or practice with words?

Word Organizer

Word: ___

Definition: ___

Part of speech (noun, verb, adjective, or adverb): ___

Synonyms: ___

Antonyms: ___

Sentence: ___

(Available online.)

-oat words		
boat	bloat	afloat
coat	**float**	lifeboat
goat	gloat	overcoat
moat	throat	**raincoat**
		riverboat
		rowboat

Smelly Sock

1st Voice	All Together	2nd Voice
Let's write about my hollyhock, the prettiest flower on my block.		
		I'd rather write about my sock. My sock will send you into shock!
Hollyhock!		
On my block!		
		Smelly sock!
		Into shock!
	We must decide by four o'clock.	
Everyone loves my hollyhock. Bees, birds, and butterflies flock.		
		It's almost four— ticktock— I say let's write about my sock.
Hollyhock!		
On my block!		
		Smelly sock!
		Into shock!
	Too late now. It's four o'clock.	

WORD LADDER 1
-ock

Name _____

**Read the clues. Then, write the words.
Start at the bottom and climb to the top.**

Time to Bloom

8. A device that tells time. **Change one letter.**

7. A group of birds of one kind that stay together. **Change one letter.**

6. A piece of hard material, such as wood or concrete. **Add one letter at the beginning.**

5. Something you open with a key. **Change one letter.**

4. To see with your eyes. **Change one letter.**

3. A small part or corner of a room, like a breakfast ___. **Change one letter.**

2. Something that you read. **Change one letter.**

1. A curved piece of metal or plastic used for hanging things, such as a painting. **Take away five letters.**

h o l l y h o c k

WORD LADDER 2
-ock

Name _____

Read the clues. Then, write the words.
Start at the bottom and climb to the top.

That Stinks!

9. 2nd Voice wanted to write about a smelly ___.
   Take away one letter.

8. A sudden, unpleasant surprise.
   Change the vowel.

7. A small, poorly built house.
   Add one letter.

6. A large bag for holding things.
   Change one letter.

5. A short nail with a flat, wide head.
   Change the last two letters.

4. Opposite of *short*.
   Take away one letter.

3. A part of a barn for holding a horse or other animal.
   Add two letters at the beginning.

2. Opposite of *nothing*.
   Take away two letters.

1. Opposite of *large*.
   Take away the last letter. Then, change the vowel.

smelly

MINI-LESSON
-ock

Sock Match

Objective: Children will match pictures of *-ock* words with consonants or consonant blends.

Materials
- "Smelly Sock" (page 94)
- highlighters
- chart paper
- pair of large socks
- Letter cards for *d, l, r, s, bl, cl, fl,* and *sm* (see right)
- Picture cards of *-ock* words (see right)

Sock Match

(Available online.)

Procedure
1. Invite children to read the poem several times.
2. Have children highlight the words with *-ock* in the poem.
3. Ask them to help brainstorm more words with the *-ock* phonogram. (See table at right for ideas.) List their words on chart paper, where children can view them.
4. Place the picture cards in one sock and the letter cards in the other sock.
5. Invite a pair of children to reach in and pick a picture card and a letter card. Ask them if the picture matches the beginning sound on the card (for example, the sock picture and the *s* card). If the cards do not match (for example, the sock picture and the *l* card), have the children hold on to the cards they picked.
6. Invite two other children to pick cards. If their picture and letter cards do not match, have the children check whether their cards match any of the previous picks. For example, if the second pair of children picks the picture of the lock and the *sm* card, their picture card would match with the previously picked *l* card. Have children with matching cards stand together.
7. Continue play until all matches are made.
8. Leave the card-filled socks at a workstation for children to use as a matching game during independent work time.

-ock words		
dock	**block**	hammock
lock	chock	hemlock
mock	clock	**hollyhock**
rock	crock	**o'clock**
sock	**flock**	padlock
tock	frock	peacock
	knock	unlock
	shock	
	smock	
	stock	

Assessment: Are children able to correctly identify the beginning sounds? Who had difficulty matching the pictures and sounds?

An Artichoke Joke

1st Voice

One day there was an artichoke . . .

He walked into a store and spoke . . .

He said to the man,
"I'm sort of broke . . ."

"But I want to buy an artichoke."

The man looked at the artichoke
and said, "It's funny that you spoke!"

You can't do much with an artichoke.

2nd Voice

Is this another corny joke?

I knew it! I think I'm going to choke.

Oh, good grief! I'm going to croak.

Why would he want an artichoke?
He already was an artichoke!
I can't believe your silly joke.

That's all there is? That's all the joke?

WORD LADDER 1
-oke

Name _____

Read the clues. Then, write the words.
Start at the bottom and climb to the top.

Eat Your Veggies

9. A place where you can buy things. **Change one letter.**

8. To look directly at something for a long time. **Change one letter.**

7. A pointed stick that can be pushed into the ground. **Change one letter.**

6. A raised platform used for plays or other performances. **Take away one letter. Add two letters in its place.**

5. Great anger. **Change one letter.**

4. A garden tool used to collect fallen leaves. **Take away one letter.**

3. A part of a car used for stopping or slowing down. **Change one letter.**

2. To have no money. **Change the first two letters.**

1. To have trouble breathing because something is blocking the windpipe. **Take away four letters.**

artichoke

WORD LADDER 2
-oke

Name _____

Read the clues. Then, write the words. Start at the bottom and climb to the top.

It's Not Funny

8. A word that describes the joke in the poem. **Add one letter at the end.**

7. The sweet yellow or white seeds we eat on the ears of a tall plant. **Change one letter.**

6. The center part of something, such as an apple. **Change one letter.**

5. Opposite of *less*. **Change one letter.**

4. A tiny hole in the skin where sweat comes out. **Change one letter.**

3. To push sharply, often with a finger. **Take away one letter.**

2. Part of a bicycle wheel; also, past tense of *speak*. **Change one letter.**

1. The gas you see when burning wood. **Take away one letter. Add two letters in its place.**

j o k e

MINI-LESSON
-oke

Box the Words

Objective: Children will read *-oke* words while playing a game.

Materials

- "An Artichoke Joke" (page 98)
- highlighters
- chart paper
- 4 different color markers (for each group of children)
- Box the Words game sheet (see right)

Procedure

1. Read the poem several times with children.

2. Have children highlight the *-oke* words in the poem.

3. Ask them to help brainstorm more words with the *-oke* phonogram. (See table at right for ideas.) List the words on chart paper, where children can view them.

4. Divide the class into groups of four children and give each group a Box the Words game sheet. Give each child in a group a different color marker.

5. To play, children take turns reading a word on the game sheet. If everyone in the group agrees the reader has read a word correctly, the reader uses his or her color marker to connect two dots next to the word. The goal is to eventually create a box around each word.

6. When a child connects the last two dots to draw a complete box around any word, that child can color the box in with his marker.

7. When all the words have been boxed, the child with the most colored boxes wins.

Note: You can simplify the game by creating your own sheet using only the words in the first and second columns in the table above. Repeat some words as needed to fill in the sheet.

Assessment: Circulate as children read the words and listen in for accuracy.

Box the Words

broke	poke	joke	smoke	yoke	artichoke
woke	stroke	bloke	awoke	slowpoke	spoke
choke	evoke	stoke	backstroke	invoke	revoke

(Available online.)

-oke words		
joke	bloke	**artichoke**
poke	**broke**	awoke
woke	**choke**	backstroke
yoke	smoke	evoke
	spoke	invoke
	stoke	revoke
	stroke	slowpoke

The Bird That Snored

PARTNER POEM -ore

1st Voice	**All Together**	**2nd Voice**
There was a bird		
		That loved to soar
High above		
		The sandy shore.
It didn't cheep		
		Or chirp or peep,
	But kid, that bird could roar!	
At night the bird		
		Would close its eyes,
Soaring still		
		Across the skies.
As time would creep		
		It fell asleep,
	And kid, that bird could snore!	
The sun could shine,		
		The rain could pour,
Whatever weather		
		Had in store,
The bird would soar		
		Above the shore,
	And never asked for more.	

WORD LADDER 1
-ore

Name _____

**Read the clues. Then, write the words.
Start at the bottom and climb to the top.**

Up and Away!

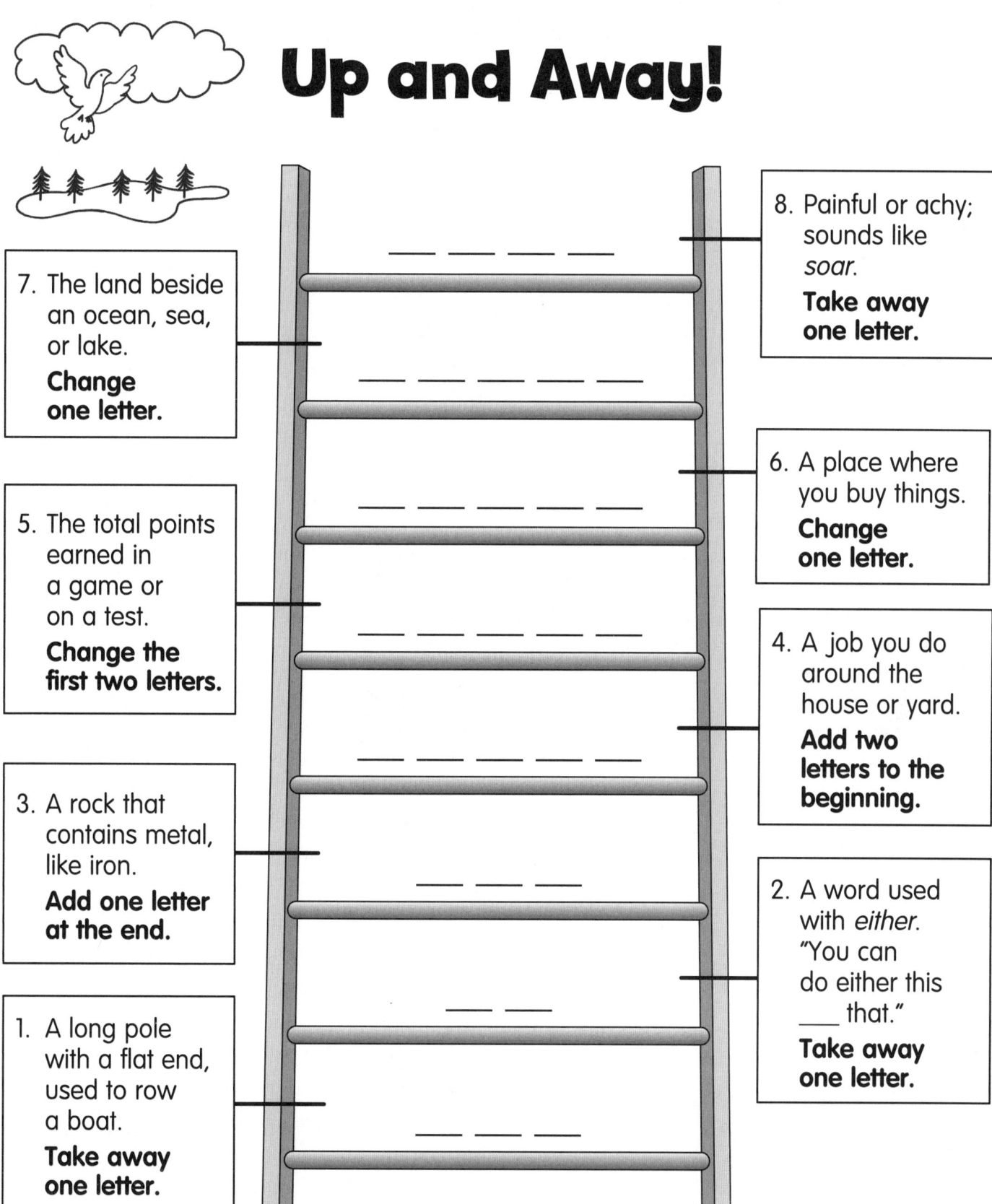

7. The land beside an ocean, sea, or lake. **Change one letter.**

5. The total points earned in a game or on a test. **Change the first two letters.**

3. A rock that contains metal, like iron. **Add one letter at the end.**

1. A long pole with a flat end, used to row a boat. **Take away one letter.**

8. Painful or achy; sounds like *soar*. **Take away one letter.**

6. A place where you buy things. **Change one letter.**

4. A job you do around the house or yard. **Add two letters to the beginning.**

2. A word used with *either*. "You can do either this ___ that." **Take away one letter.**

s o a r

WORD LADDER 2
-ore

Name _____

Read the clues. Then, write the words.
Start at the bottom and climb to the top.

Sing It!

9. Another sound made by birds. **Add one letter.**

8. A small piece of something that is broken off. **Change one letter.**

7. To cut wood with an ax. **Take away the last two letters. Add one letter in their place.**

6. A job you do around the house or yard. **Change one letter.**

5. The land beside an ocean, sea, or lake. **Take away the last letter. Add two letters in its place.**

4. A small store. **Change two letters.**

3. Sound made by a walking horse; "clip-___." **Change the two middle letters.**

2. To become rough or dry so your skin cracks; also, a friend. **Take away one letter.**

1. Not expensive. **Change one letter.**

c h e e p

MINI-LESSON
-ore

Ore Match

Objective: Children will find partners to match word parts to create an *-ore* word.

Materials
- "The Bird That Snored" (page 102)
- highlighters
- chart paper
- Ore Match cards (see right)

Ore Match

a	a	any	be	book
en	ex	folk	ga	sea
dore	shore	more	fore	store
core	plore	lore	lore	shore
ch	ore	sc	ore	sn
ore	st	ore	sh	ore

(Available online.)

Procedure

1. Invite children to read the poem several times.

2. Have children help highlight the *-ore* words in the poem.

3. Ask them to brainstorm more words with the *-ore* phonogram. (See table at right for ideas.) List these words on chart paper, where children can view them. Add any words from the table's third column that were not suggested by children.

-ore words		
bore	chore	adore
core	score	ashore
fore	**shore**	anymore
gore	**snore**	before
lore	spore	bookstore
more	**store**	encore
ore	swore	explore
pore		folklore
sore		galore
wore		seashore

4. Discuss the words, pointing out the *-ore* phonograms. If needed, discuss the words' definitions or invite children to use each word in a sentence.

5. Tell children that you will give them cards with word parts written on them. Their job is to match the cards to create words from the list.

6. Pass out the Ore Match cards to children. (The last two rows of cards combine to make words from column 2 and are a little easier to match, so strategically give these cards to children who need more support. If more support is needed, draw symbols—such as stars, Xs, or Ts—on cards that match. These symbols will give children a way to double check their work.)

7. Invite children to work together to match cards that form words. (Words are *adore, ashore, anymore, before, bookstore, chore, encore, explore, folklore, galore, score, seashore, shore, snore, store*.)

8. Leave the word chart and the Ore Match cards at a workstation for children to match during independent work time.

Assessment: Listen as children attempt to match cards to create words. How well do they blend the two cards? Are they able to correctly make *-ore* words?

Shout for Brussels Sprout

1st Voice

I've nothing good
to say about
the rubbery, stout
Brussels sprout.

2nd Voice

I disagree.
The Brussels sprout,
when served with soup
and rainbow trout,
makes a meal
worth shouting about.

I say neither
soup nor trout
can make me shout
for a Brussels sprout.

What is it you
don't get about
the zesty taste
of a Brussels sprout?

A Brussels sprout
for me strikes out.
I'd rather eat
the bathroom grout.
Make me eat it,
I will pout.

You have poor taste
without a doubt.
We all love
our Brussels sprout!

WORD LADDER 1
-out

Name _____

Read the clues. Then, write the words.
Start at the bottom and climb to the top.

Who Likes Brussels Sprouts?

8. To push out the lips to show anger or disappointment. **Change one letter.**

7. A place where ships dock to load and unload cargo. **Take away one letter.**

6. A game in which players do physical activity. **Change one letter.**

5. Opposite of *tall*. **Change one letter.**

4. A loud sound made by forcing air through the nose. **Change one letter.**

3. The long front part of a pig's head; includes the nose and mouth. **Change one letter.**

2. To call out in a loud voice. **Change one letter.**

1. "The itsy-bitsy spider went up the water ___." **Take away one letter.**

s p r o u t

WORD LADDER 2
-out

Name _____

Read the clues. Then, write the words.
Start at the bottom and climb to the top.

Yummy!

9. 2nd Voice thinks the Brussels sprout has a zesty ___.
Change one letter.

8. A soft mixture used to stick things together.
Add one letter at the end.

7. What happened yesterday is in the ___.
Change one letter.

6. A pole that's stuck in the ground to support something.
Move the letters around.

5. A small mark or stain.
Take away one letter.

4. A tube or pipe through which liquid flows.
Add one letter at the beginning.

3. To push out the lips to show unhappiness.
Change the middle two letters.

2. A bug that causes problems, like destroying plants.
Change one letter.

1. A set of questions to find out how much someone knows.
Change the first letter. Take away the last letter.

z e s t y

108

Shout It Out

MINI-LESSON *-out*

Objective: Children will respond to a prompt with an *-out* rhyming word.

Materials
- "Shout for Brussels Sprout" (page 106)
- highlighters
- chart paper
- pencils or pens
- 12 Shout It Out megaphones (see right)

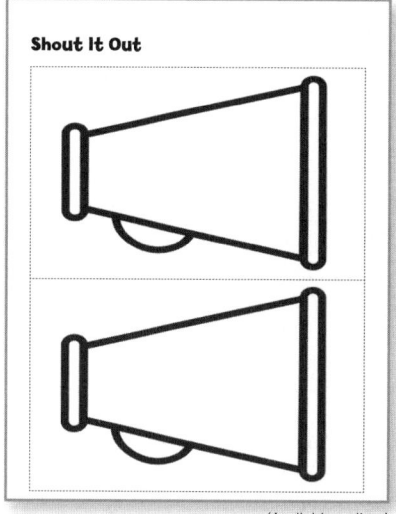

(Available online.)

Procedure
1. Read the poem several times with children.
2. Have children highlight all the *-out* words in the poem.
3. Ask children to brainstorm more words with the *-out* phonogram. (See table below for ideas.) List these words on chart paper, where children can view them.
4. Divide the class into two teams and give each team six blank megaphones. Have each team work together to write six *-out* words from the poem or brainstormed list, one on each megaphone. Make sure the megaphones are distributed among team members. (Some children may need to share one.)
5. To play the game, ask the first team to give a clue about one of their words. For example, they might give a definition, such as, "This is a vegetable." Or, from the poem: "This is what 1st Voice did not want to eat."
6. Anyone on the other team can "shout" out the answer. If they are correct, their team gets the megaphone with the word. If incorrect, the team giving the clue gets to keep the megaphone.
7. After clues have been given for all 12 words, the team with the most megaphones wins.

-out words		
bout	clout	**about**
gout	flout	**Brussels sprout**
lout	**grout**	dugout
out	scout	hideout
pout	shout	
	snout	
	spout	
	sprout	
	stout	
	trout	

Assessment: Listen to the clues given by team members. How well do they define the word with a clue or context sentence?

Rats, I Forgot!

1st Voice	**2nd Voice**
Hello, I'm Joe.	
	My name's Flo.
I want to tell you something, Flo.	
	Fine, Joe. Let's go.
Once, a long, long time ago . . .	
	How long, Joe?
I don't know. Long time ago.	
	Okay. So?
Now I don't remember, Flo.	
	Was it too long, long ago?
I don't know.	
	Start over, Joe.
Hello, I'm Joe.	
	My name's Flo.
Once, a long, long time ago . . .	

(continued)

PARTNER POEM
-ow (long sound)

1st Voice	**2nd Voice**
	Forget again?
Afraid so.	
	Was it about your hair, Joe?
	Your ear?
	Elbow?
I don't know.	
	Maybe about the rain, Joe?
	Hail?
	Snow?
Don't think so, Flo.	
	Maybe a long, long time ago
	your daddy took you to a show.
No, it wasn't about a show.	
Might have been a crow, though.	
I just don't know.	
	Start over, Joe.
Hello, I'm Joe.	
	My name's Flo.
Once, a long, long time ago . . .	

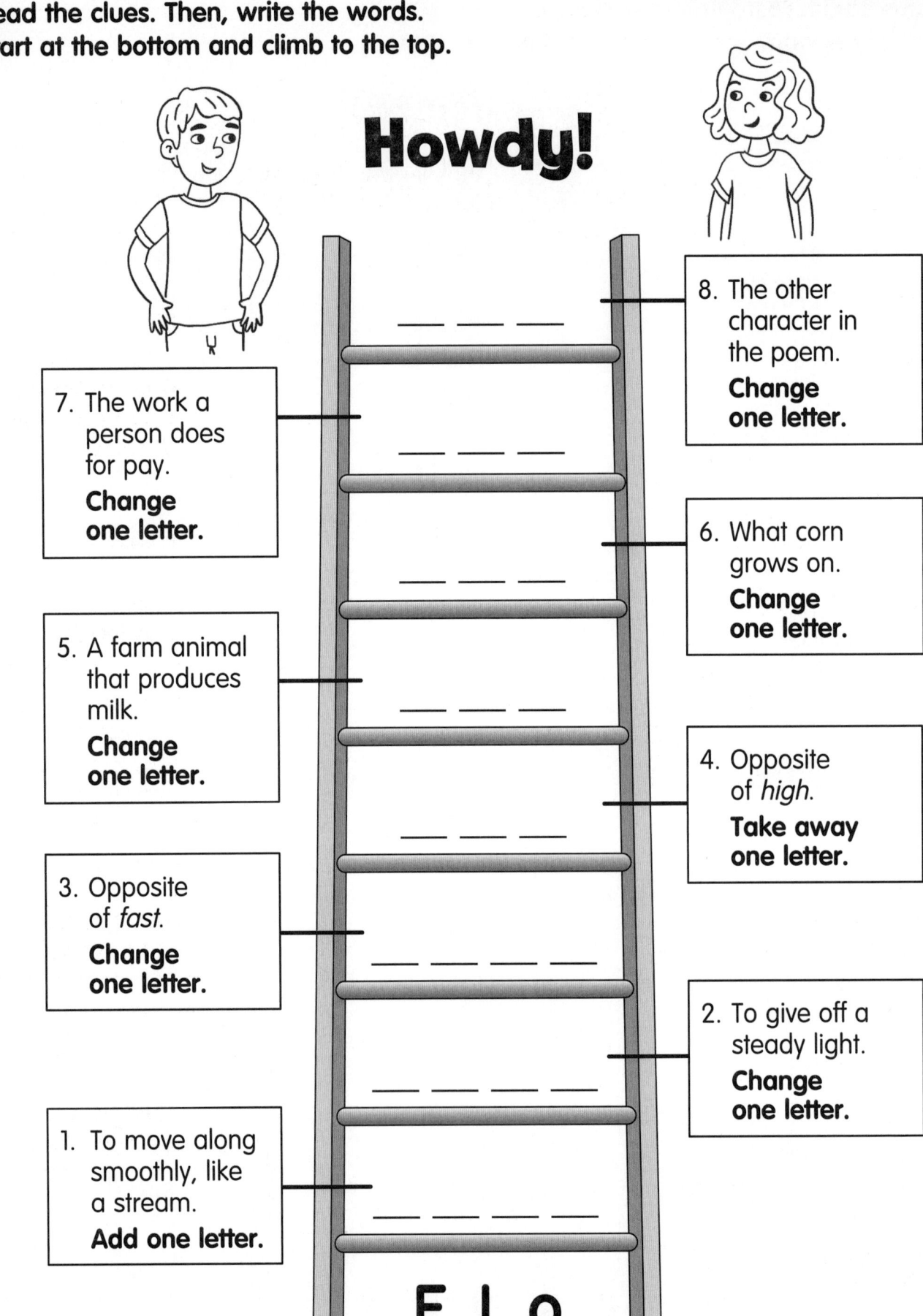

Name _____

WORD LADDER 2
-ow (long sound)

Read the clues. Then, write the words.
Start at the bottom and climb to the top.

Start at the Beginning

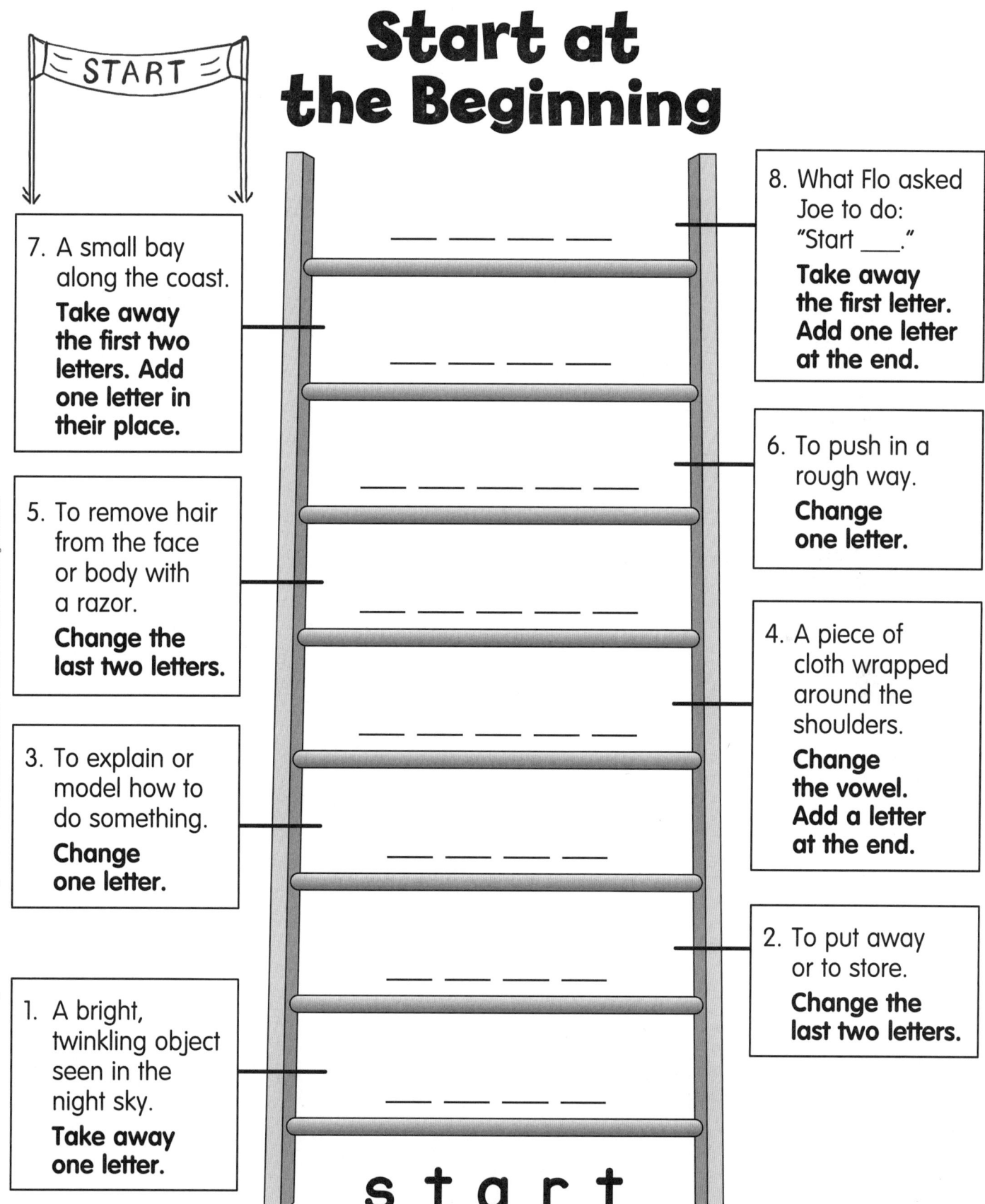

7. A small bay along the coast. **Take away the first two letters. Add one letter in their place.**

8. What Flo asked Joe to do: "Start ___." **Take away the first letter. Add one letter at the end.**

6. To push in a rough way. **Change one letter.**

5. To remove hair from the face or body with a razor. **Change the last two letters.**

4. A piece of cloth wrapped around the shoulders. **Change the vowel. Add a letter at the end.**

3. To explain or model how to do something. **Change one letter.**

2. To put away or to store. **Change the last two letters.**

1. A bright, twinkling object seen in the night sky. **Take away one letter.**

s t a r t

MINI-LESSON
-ow (long sound)

Roll for -ow Words

Objective: Children will roll dice to create *-ow* words.

Materials

- "Rats, I Forgot!" (page 110)
- highlighters
- chart paper
- 2 dice (for each small group)
- pencils or pens
- Roll for *-ow* Words game sheet (see right)

Procedure

1. Read the poem several times with children.

2. Have children help highlight the *-ow* words in the poem.

3. Ask them to help brainstorm more words with the *-ow* phonogram. (See table below for ideas.) List these words on chart paper, where children can view them.

4. Divide the class into small groups of four or five children. Give each group a pair of dice, and give each child a game sheet.

5. To play, children take turns rolling the dice. The number that comes up determines which *-ow* word they will make, as per the first column of the game sheet. For example, say a child rolls a 9. The child then says, "The word is *crow*," and writes *cr* in the space in the second column to make the word (9 = *cr*; *crow*).

6. As play continues, if a child rolls a number that has already come up, he or she skips a turn. The bottom box is a wild space. Children can use this space at any time to write any other *-ow* words. (For example, they can write one of the words from the third column of the table.) The first child to fill in all 12 spaces wins.

Roll for -ow Words

2 = b	_____ow
3 = l	_____ow
4 = m	_____ow
5 = r	_____ow
6 = s	_____ow
7 = kn	_____ow
8 = bl	_____ow
9 = cr	_____ow
10 = fl	_____ow
11 = sh	_____ow
12 = thr	_____ow
? = ? (wild space)	_____ow

(Available online.)

-ow words (long sound)		
bow	blow	aglow
low	**crow**	arrow
mow	flow	below
row	glow	bestow
sow	grow	burrow
tow	**know**	**elbow**
	show	fellow
	slow	wallow
	snow	widow
	throw	

Assessment: Listen as children play the game. Are they correctly blending the *-ow* words?

It's Too Late Now

1st Voice	2nd Voice	3rd Voice
Why does a dog bow-wow-wow instead of moo like a cow?		
	Why does a cat meow-meow instead of grunt like a sow?	
		Who decides who grunts or moos or meows or goes bow-wow?
I guess it works.		
	Still somehow,	
		It might be fun for a cow to meow
A sow to moo or bow-wow-wow,		
	But it's much too late to change it now.	

Name _____

WORD LADDER 1
-ow (short sound)

Read the clues. Then, write the words.
Start at the bottom and climb to the top.

Did You Hear That Sound?

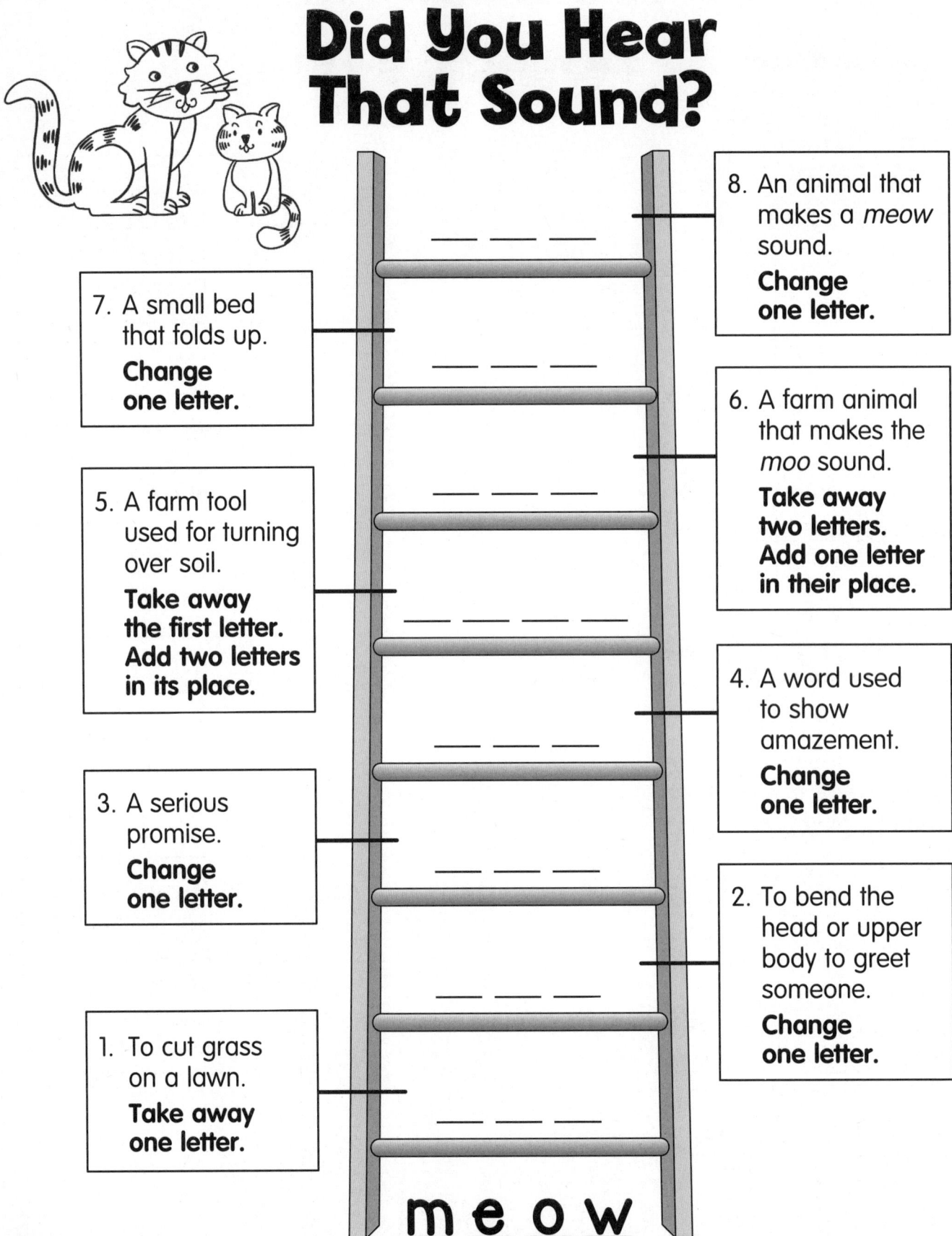

8. An animal that makes a *meow* sound.
   Change one letter.

7. A small bed that folds up.
   Change one letter.

6. A farm animal that makes the *moo* sound.
   Take away two letters. Add one letter in their place.

5. A farm tool used for turning over soil.
   Take away the first letter. Add two letters in its place.

4. A word used to show amazement.
   Change one letter.

3. A serious promise.
   Change one letter.

2. To bend the head or upper body to greet someone.
   Change one letter.

1. To cut grass on a lawn.
   Take away one letter.

m e o w

WORD LADDER 2
-ow (short sound)

Name _____

Read the clues. Then, write the words. Start at the bottom and climb to the top.

Hog Out

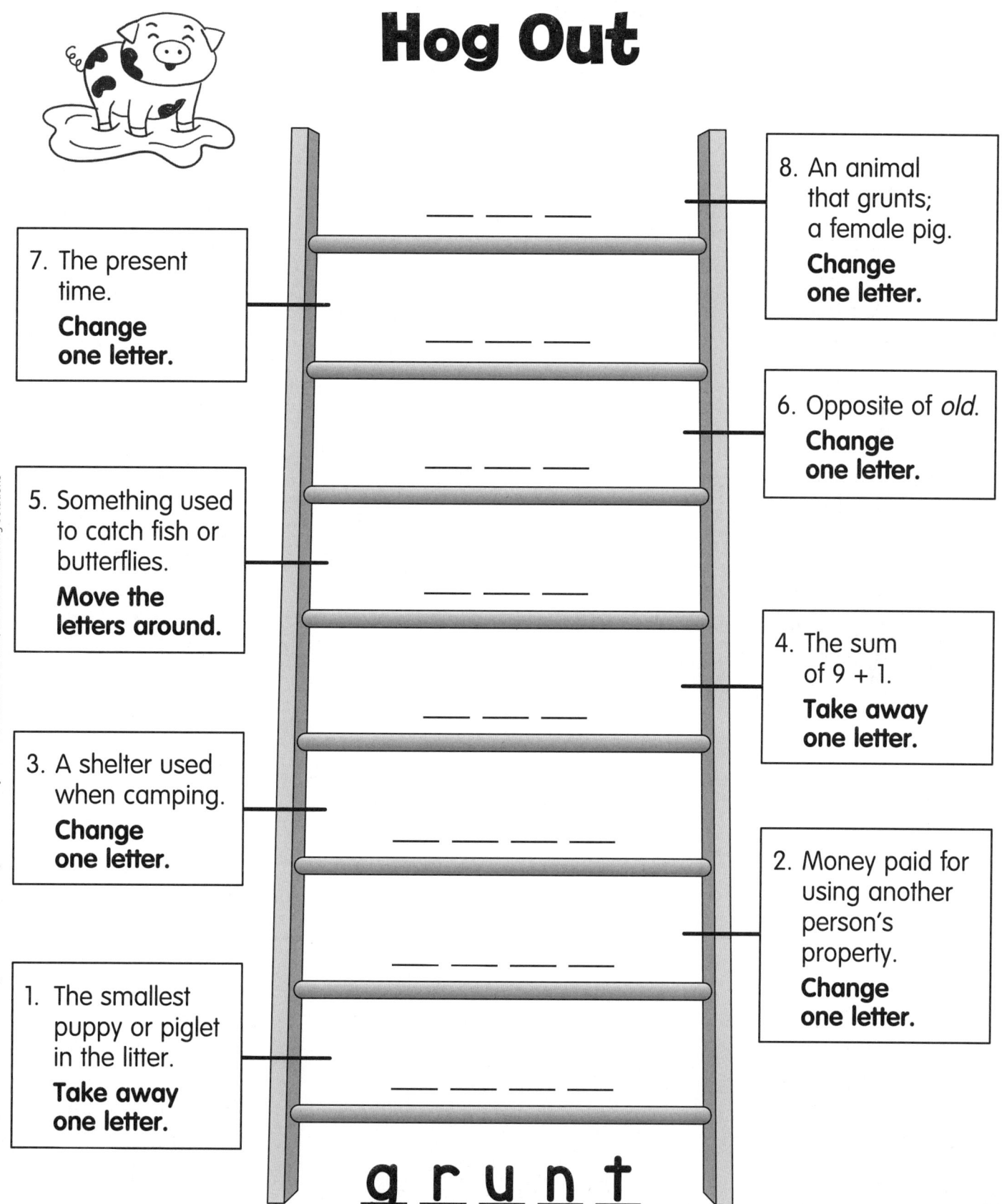

8. An animal that grunts; a female pig. **Change one letter.**

7. The present time. **Change one letter.**

6. Opposite of *old*. **Change one letter.**

5. Something used to catch fish or butterflies. **Move the letters around.**

4. The sum of 9 + 1. **Take away one letter.**

3. A shelter used when camping. **Change one letter.**

2. Money paid for using another person's property. **Change one letter.**

1. The smallest puppy or piglet in the litter. **Take away one letter.**

g r u n t

MINI-LESSON
-ow (short sound)

Ow Swat

Objective: Children will recognize the two sounds of *-ow*.

Materials

- "It's Too Late Now" (page 115)
- highlighters
- chart paper
- 2 flyswatters (real or made from cardboard)
- Ow Swat word cards* (see right)
- tape

* To prepare, cut apart the Ow Swat words and tape them up around the room or on the front wall.

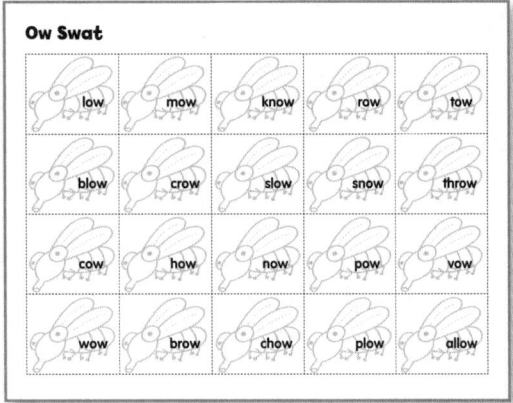

(Available online.)

Procedure

1. Invite children to read the poem several times.
2. Have children highlight the *-ow* words in the poem.
3. Ask them to help brainstorm more words with the *-ow* phonogram. (See table at right for ideas.) List these words on chart paper, where children can view them.
4. Remind children of the long *-ow* sound words from the previous poem. Talk about the two sounds of *-ow*.
5. Divide the class into two teams and have each team line up. Give the first child in each line a flyswatter.
6. Explain that you will call out a word and children must find a "rhyming fly" on the wall and swat it with their flyswatter. For instance, if you say *cow*, children should look for a short *-ow* word to swat. Conversely, if you say *snow*, they should look for a long *-ow* word to swat.
7. Ask the child who swatted a word first to read it. If the child correctly reads the word and it is a rhyming fly, her team wins a point.
8. Continue play until children have swatted all the words on the wall.
9. Leave the Ow Swat words at a workstation. Invite children to sort them by long and short *-ow* sounds during independent work time.

-ow words		
bow	brow	allow
cow	chow	anyhow
how	plow	endow
now		**meow**
pow		powwow
sow		prowl
vow		**somehow**
wow		

Assessment: Are children able to recognize and identify the two different *-ow* sounds? Who had difficulty?

PARTNER POEM
-oon/-ook/-oom

Eat the Moon

1st Voice (-oon)	2nd Voice (-ook)	3rd Voice (-oom)
Have you seen the moon tonight?		
	Hurry! Look!	
		An orange ball. *A flower in bloom.*
A huge balloon.		
	Something good enough to cook.	
I have a spoon.		
	We need a hook.	
		Eat the moon, we'll be in gloom.
I guess you're right.		
	One last look.	
		The moon will zoom,
Be gone soon.		
	Over brook,	
		Sleeping loom, Sail off over
Sea and dune.		
	Tonight, have you	
Seen the moon?		
Hurry! Hurry! Hurry!	Hurry! Hurry! Hurry!	*Hurry! Hurry! Hurry!*

WORD LADDER 1
-oon/-ook/-oom

Name _____

**Read the clues. Then, write the words.
Start at the bottom and climb to the top.**

Night Sky

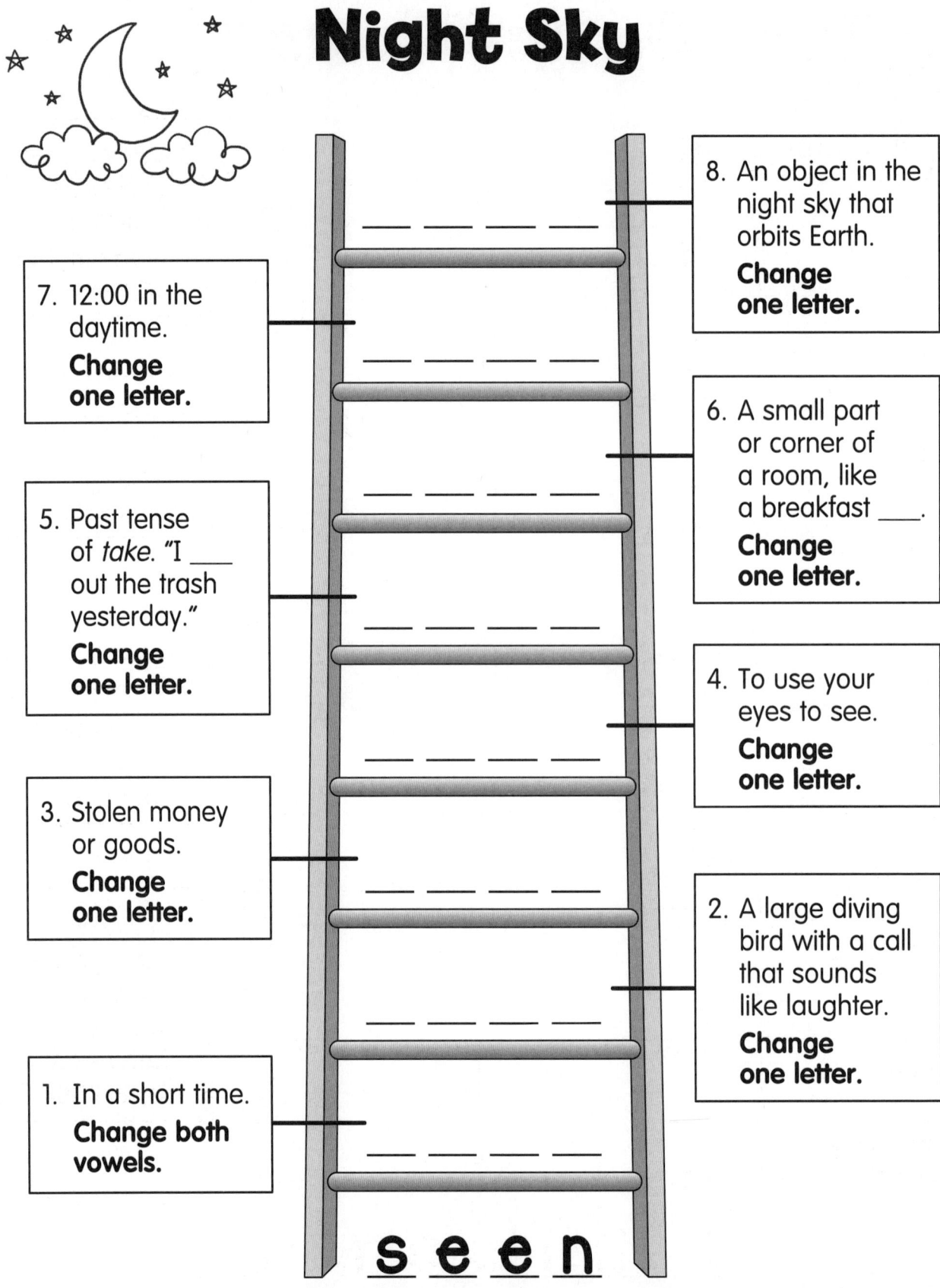

8. An object in the night sky that orbits Earth. **Change one letter.**

7. 12:00 in the daytime. **Change one letter.**

6. A small part or corner of a room, like a breakfast ___. **Change one letter.**

5. Past tense of *take*. "I ___ out the trash yesterday." **Change one letter.**

4. To use your eyes to see. **Change one letter.**

3. Stolen money or goods. **Change one letter.**

2. A large diving bird with a call that sounds like laughter. **Change one letter.**

1. In a short time. **Change both vowels.**

s e e n

Name _____

WORD LADDER 2
-oon/-ook/-oom

Read the clues. Then, write the words.
Start at the bottom and climb to the top.

Out in Bloom

8. What a plant makes when it blooms. **Add two letters at the end.**

7. To move along smoothly, like a river or stream. **Add one letter at the beginning.**

6. Opposite of *high*. **Change one letter.**

5. To use oars to move a boat on water. **Take away two letters. Add one letter in their place.**

4. Part of a house that has its own walls and door. **Take away one letter.**

3. Used for sweeping floors. **Change two letters.**

2. A feeling of sadness and hopelessness. **Add one letter at the beginning.**

1. A machine for weaving cloth. **Take away one letter.**

b l o o m

MINI-LESSON
-oon/-ook/-oom

Grab Bag Buddies

Objective: Children will provide a word that uses the *oo* phonogram selected during a game.

Materials
- "Eat the Moon" (page 119)
- highlighters
- chart paper
- paper bag (or tote bag)
- paper and pencils
- timer
- *-oon, -ook, -oom* phonogram cards (see right)

Grab Bag Buddies

-oon	-ook	-oom
-oon	-ook	-oom
-oon	-ook	-oom
-oon	-ook	-oom
-oon	-ook	-oom

(Available online.)

Procedure
1. Invite children to read the poem several times.
2. Have children highlight the words with *oo* in the poem. Guide them to recognize that there are three phonograms: *-oon, -ook,* and *-oom*.
3. Ask them to help brainstorm more words for each phonogram. (See table at right for ideas.) List these words on chart paper, making three columns, one for each *oo* phonogram. Put the chart where children can view them.
4. Place the phonogram cards in a paper bag.
5. Pair up children to make two-person teams. Give each pair paper and pencils.
6. Pass the bag, inviting one child from each team to select a card. Tell children that they will write as many words as they can think of that contains their selected phonogram. (You may choose to hide the chart that you made together at the beginning of the lesson.)

-oon/-ook/-oom words		
-oon (long oo)	**-ook (short oo)**	**-oom (long oo)**
goon	book	boom
loon	**cook**	doom
moon	hook	**loom**
noon	**look**	zoom
soon	nook	broom
croon	rook	**bloom**
spoon	took	**gloom**
baboon	**brook**	groom
balloon	crook	bathroom
lagoon	shook	bedroom
maroon	notebook	classroom
racoon	outlook	heirloom
teaspoon		
tycoon		

7. Set the timer from 30 seconds to 2 minutes, depending on children's needs. When time is up, have teams with the same *oo* phonogram get together and compare their lists.
8. Invite children from each *oo* phonogram group share their words with the rest of the class.

Assessment: Circulate as children work to create their word lists. How well do they rhyme the word and think of ones that contained their *oo* phonogram?

References

Bridgeland, J., & Bruce, M. (2013). *The missing piece: A national teacher survey on how social and emotional learning can empower children and transform schools.* Collaborative for Academic, Social, and Emotional Learning.

Fresch, M. J. (2019). Poetry across the curriculum: An approach for learning vocabulary and content. *Missouri Reader, 42*(2), 14–17.

Fry, E. (1998). The most common phonograms. *The Reading Teacher, 51,* 620–622.

Gill, S. R. (2007). The forgotten genre of children's poetry. *The Reading Teacher, 60,* 622–625.

Menon, S., & Hiebert, E. H. (2005). A comparison of first graders' reading with little books or literature-based basal anthologies. *Reading Research Quarterly, 40*(1), 12–38.

Online Etymology Dictionary. https://www.etymoline.com.

Perfect, K. A. (1999). Rhyme and reason: Poetry for the heart and head. *The Reading Teacher, 52,* 728–737.

Pierce, L. (2011). *Repeated readings in poetry versus prose: Fluency and enjoyment for second graders.* [Unpublished doctoral dissertation]. University of Toledo.

Rasinski, T. (2008). *Daily word ladders: Grades 1–2.* Scholastic.

Rasinski, T. (2012). *Daily word ladders: Grades K–1.* Scholastic.

Rasinski, T. (2020, September 12). Why poetry? Let me count the ways. *The Robb Review.* https://therobbreviewblog.com/uncategorized/poetry/.

Rasinski, T., Harrison, D. L., & Fawcett, G. (2009). *Partner poems for building fluency.* Scholastic.

Rasinski, T., Rupley, W. H., & Nichols, W. D. (2012). *Phonics and fluency practice with poetry.* Scholastic.

Rasinski, T., & Stevenson, B. (2005). The effects of fast start reading, a fluency-based home involvement reading program, on the reading achievement of beginning readers. *Reading Psychology: An International Quarterly, 26,* 109–125.

Rasinski, T. V., & Zimmerman, B. (2013). What's the perfect text for struggling readers? Try poetry! *Reading Today, 30,* 15–16.

Rasinski, T. V., & Zimmerman, B. (2015, July). Guest-edited issue of the *New England Reading Association Journal* devoted to poetry.

Seitz, S. (2013). Poetic fluency. *The Reading Teacher, 67,* 312–314.

Shanahan, T. (2016, June 26). Further explanation of teaching students with challenging text. *Shanahan on Literacy.* Accessed at https://shanahanonliteracy.com/blog/further-explanation-of-teaching-students-with-challenging-text.

Stahl, S., & Heubach, K. (2005). Fluency-oriented reading instruction. *Journal of Literacy Research, 37,* 25–60.

Wilfong, L. G. (2008). Building fluency, word-recognition ability, and confidence in struggling readers: The poetry academy. *The Reading Teacher, 62*(1), 4–13.

Wylie, R. E., & Durrell, D. D. (1970). Teaching vowels through phonograms. *Elementary School Journal, 47,* 787–791.

Word Ladder Template

Read the clues. Then, write the words.
Start at the bottom and climb to the top.

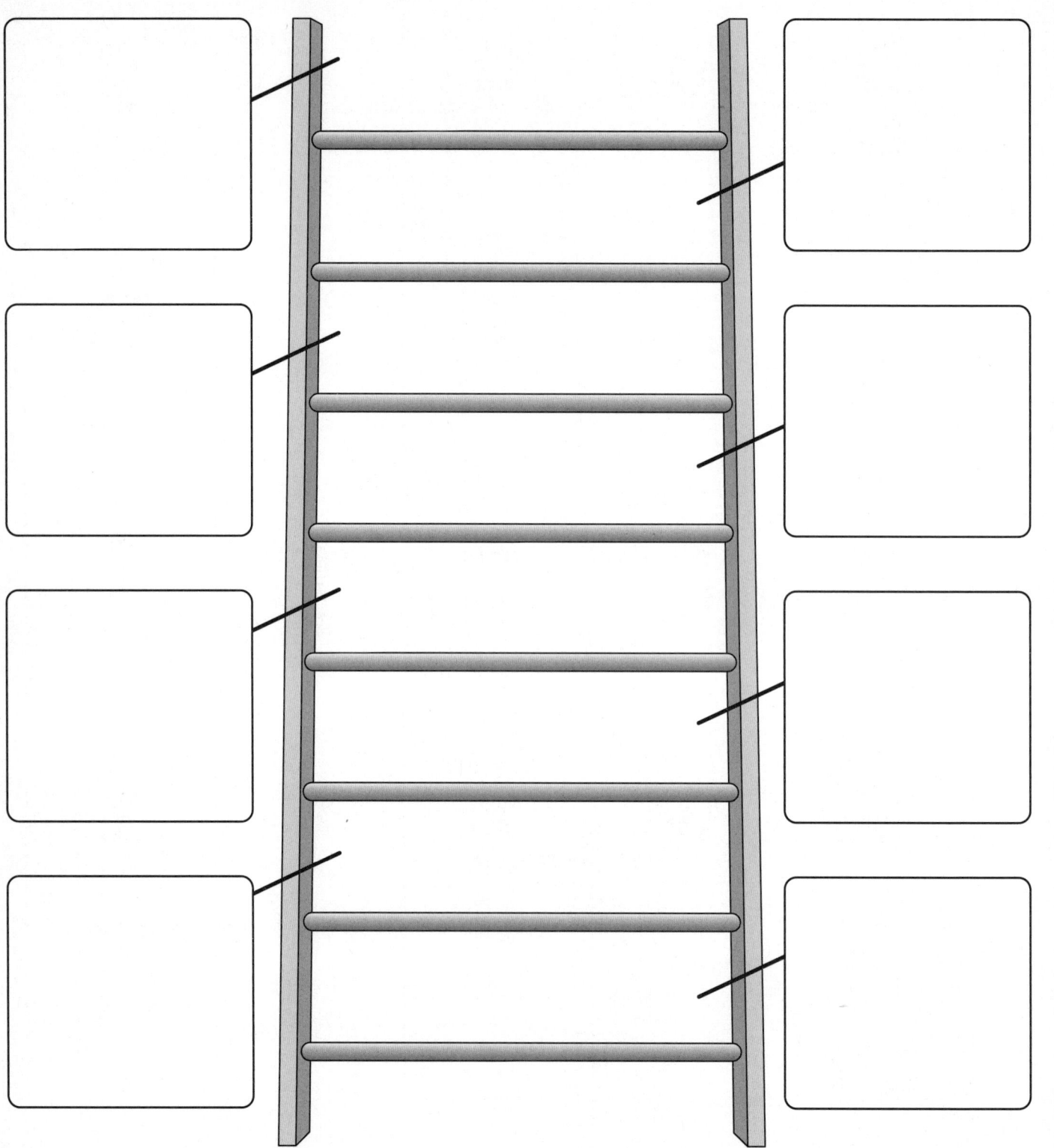

Consonant Letter Cards

b	c	d	f	g
h	j	k	l	m
n	p	r	s	t
v	w	x	y	z
qu				

Consonant Cluster Cards

bl	br	cl
cr	dr	fl
fr	gl	gr
pl	pr	sc
sk	sl	sm

sn	sp	spl
spr	st	str
sw	tr	tw
ch	ph	sh
th	wh	

Answer Key (Word Ladders)

-ail
page 13: 1. nail 2. tail 3. tall 4. mall 5. mail 6. sail 7. pail 8. Gail
page 14: 1. quail 2. trail 3. mail 4. main 5. maid 6. mad 7. tad 8. toad 9. road

-ain
page 17: 1. Spain 2. spin 3. chin 4. chain 5. stain 6. brain 7. plain 8. pain
page 18: 1. lane 2. mane 3. man 4. pan 5. pane 6. plane 7. plan 8. plain 9. complain

-ake
page 22: 1. stake 2. take 3. bake 4. bike 5. like 6. lake 7. lace 8. face 9. fake
page 23: 1. cake 2. take 3. mistake 4. make 5. lake 6. lame 7. flame 8. flake 9. snowflake

-ale
page 26: 1. scale 2. stale 3. tale 4. pale 5. pal 6. pan 7. tan 8. ton
page 27: 1. fold 2. mold 3. mole 4. male 5. female 6. mate 7. date 8. dale 9. tale

-ame
page 31: 1. lame 2. name 3. nay 4. day 5. May 6. say 7. same 8. shame
page 32: 1. float 2. flat 3. flame 4. lame 5. tame 6. mate 7. meat 8. great

-ash
page 35: 1. hush 2. shush 3. rush 4. crush 5. crash 6. trash 7. rash 8. lash
page 36: 1. lap 2. lamp 3. lump 4. lunch 5. munch 6. much 7. mush 8. mash 9. dash

-ate
page 40: 1. late 2. hate 3. hat 4. hot 5. how 6. show 7. chow 8. cow
page 41: 1. pen 2. men 3. man 4. mad 5. made 6. maze 7. gaze 8. gate 9. grate

-aw
page 44: 1. row 2. raw 3. paw 4. pow 5. low 6. law 7. jaw 8. caw
page 45: 1. burn 2. bun 3. run 4. ran 5. raw 6. draw 7. haw 8. ham

-eat
page 48: 1. rack 2. race 3. ace 4. ate 5. eat 6. treat 7. meat 8. seat
page 49: 1. map 2. mat 3. meat 4. cheat 5. heat 6. hot 7. plot 8. plow 9. pillow

-eed
page 53: 1. deed 2. need 3. weed 4. wed 5. red 6. Fred 7. freed 8. feed
page 54: 1. cent 2. sent 3. seed 4. sod 5. sob 6. rob 7. throb 8. broth 9. brother

-ell
page 58: 1. spell 2. swell 3. well 4. wall 5. tall 6. stall 7. small 8. smell
page 59: 1. dell 2. well 3. sell 4. bell 5. bill 6. gill 7. give 8. hive 9. alive

-est
page 62: 1. boy 2. joy 3. jay 4. bay 5. bat 6. bet 7. best 8. vest 9. west
page 63: 1. rat 2. vat 3. vast 4. vest 5. pest 6. step 7. snap 8. snake

-ew
page 66: 1. blue 2. blew 3. flew 4. few 5. dew 6. drew 7. crew 8. grew
page 67: 1. bit 2. bet 3. pet 4. pew 5. dew 6. sew 7. stew 8. chew

-ice
page 70: 1. rice 2. race 3. lace 4. lane 5. line 6. pine 7. dine 8. dice 9. nice
page 71: 1. spice 2. space 3. race 4. rage 5. page 6. age 7. sage 8. sane 9. insane

-ick
page 74: 1. trick 2. truck 3. stuck 4. stack 5. stick 6. slick 7. lick 8. sick
page 75: 1. nice 2. nick 3. trick 4. Rick 5. rack 6. ram 7. cram 8. cream

-ide
page 78: 1. hide 2. pride 3. ride 4. tide 5. tire 6. fire 7. fare 8. far
page 79: 1. clue 2. true 3. tire 4. tide 5. side 6. wide 7. wise 8. wish 9. fish

-ight
page 82: 1. night 2. right 3. bright 4. fright 5. fit 6. fat 7. far 8. star
page 83: 1. dish 2. fish 3. fight 4. flight 5. slight 6. sight 7. night 8. tonight

-ine
page 86: 1. care 2. cane 3. lane 4. pane 5. pine 6. spine 7. fine 8. fish
page 87: 1. mine 2. shine 3. whine 4. wine 5. win 6. won 7. worn 8. worm

-oat
page 91: 1. goat 2. float 3. coat 4. cat 5. cot 6. cod 7. cow 8. row
page 92: 1. gloat 2. throat 3. oat 4. out 5. pout 6. point 7. paint 8. pain 9. rain

-ock
page 95: 1. hook 2. book 3. nook 4. look 5. lock 6. block 7. flock 8. clock
page 96: 1. small 2. all 3. stall 4. tall 5. tack 6. sack 7. shack 8. shock 9. sock

-oke
page 99: 1. choke 2. broke 3. brake 4. rake 5. rage 6. stage 7. stake 8. stare 9. store
page 100: 1. smoke 2. spoke 3. poke 4. pore 5. more 6. core 7. corn 8. corny

-ore
page 103: 1. oar 2. or 3. ore 4. chore 5. score 6. store 7. shore 8. sore
page 104: 1. cheap 2. chap 3. clop 4. shop 5. shore 6. chore 7. chop 8. chip 9. chirp

-out
page 107: 1. spout 2. shout 3. snout 4. snort 5. short 6. sport 7. port 8. pout
page 108: 1. test 2. pest 3. pout 4. spout 5. spot 6. post 7. past 8. paste 9. taste

-ow (long sound)
page 112: 1. flow 2. glow 3. slow 4. low 5. cow 6. cob 7. job 8. Joe
page 113: 1. star 2. stow 3. show 4. shawl 5. shave 6. shove 7. cove 8. over

-ow (short sound)
page 116: 1. mow 2. bow 3. vow 4. wow 5. plow 6. cow 7. cot 8. cat
page 117: 1. runt 2. rent 3. tent 4. ten 5. net 6. new 7. now 8. sow

-oon/-ook/-oom
page 120: 1. soon 2. loon 3. loot 4. look 5. took 6. nook 7. noon 8. moon
page 121: 1. loom 2. gloom 3. broom 4. room 5. row 6. low 7. flow 8. flower